The World According to Clarkson

JEREMY CLARKSON

PENGUIN BOOKS

PENGUIN BOOKS

Published by the Penguin Group
Penguin Books Ltd, 80 Strand, London WC2R ORL, England
Penguin Group (USA) Inc., 375 Hudson Street, New York, New York 10014, USA
Penguin Group (Canada), 10 Alcorn Avenue, Toronto, Ontario, Canada M4V 3B2
(a division of Pearson Penguin Canada Inc.)
Penguin Ireland, 25 St Stephen's Green, Dublin 2, Ireland
(a division of Penguin Books Ltd)
Penguin Group (Australia), 250 Camberwell Road,
Camberwell, Victoria 3124, Australia (a division of Pearson Australia Group Pty Ltd)
Penguin Books India Pvt Ltd, 11 Community Centre,
Panchsheel Park, New Delhi – 110 017, India
Penguin Group (NZ), cnr Airborne and Rosedale Roads, Albany,
Auckland 1310, New Zealand (a division of Pearson New Zealand Ltd)
Penguin Books (South Africa) (Pty) Ltd, 24 Sturdee Avenue,
Rosebank 2196, South Africa

Penguin Books Ltd, Registered Offices: 80 Strand, London WC2R ORL, England

www.penguin.com

These articles first appeared in the *Sunday Times* between 2001 and 2003
This collection first published by Michael Joseph 2004
Published in Penguin Books 2005

11

Copyright © Jeremy Clarkson, 2004
All rights reserved.

The moral right of the author has been asserted

Set by Rowland Phototypesetting Ltd, Bury St Edmunds, Suffolk
Printed in England by Clays Ltd, St Ives plc

To Francie

Contents

Another Day's Holiday? Please, Give Me a Break

According to a poll, the vast majority of people questioned as they struggled back to work last week thought that England should have followed Scotland's lead and made Tuesday a bank holiday.

Two things strike me as odd here. First, that anyone could be bothered to undertake such research and, second, that anyone in their right mind could think that the Christmas break was in some way too short.

I took ten days off and by 11 o'clock on the first morning I had drunk fourteen cups of coffee, read all the newspapers and the *Guardian* and then . . . and then what?

By lunchtime I was so bored that I decided to hang a few pictures. So I found a hammer, and later a man came to replaster the bits of wall I had demolished. Then I tried to fix the electric gates, which work only when there's an omega in the month. So I went down the drive with a spanner, and later another man came to put them back together again.

I was just about to start on the Aga, which had broken down on Christmas Eve, as they do, when my wife took me on one side by my earlobe and explained that builders do not, on the whole, spend their spare time writing, so writers should not build on their days off. It's expensive and it can be dangerous, she said.

She's right. We have these lights in the dining room which are supposed to project stars onto the table below. It has never really bothered me that the light seeps out of the sides so the stars are invisible; but when you are bored, this is exactly the sort of thing that gets on your nerves.

So I bought some gaffer tape and suddenly my life had a purpose. There was something to do.

Mercifully, Christmas intervened before I could do any more damage, but then it went away again and once more I found myself staring at the day through the wrong end of a pair of binoculars. Each morning, bed and the blessed relief of unconsciousness seemed so far away.

I wore a groove in the kitchen floor with endless trips to the fridge, hoping against hope that I had somehow missed a plateful of cold sausages on the previous 4,000 excursions. Then, for no obvious reason, I decided to buy a footstool.

I took the entire family to the sort of gifty-wifty shop where the smell of pot-pourri is so pungent that it makes you go cross-eyed. Even though the children were lying on the floor gagging, I still spent hours deliberately choosing a footstool that was too small and the wrong colour so that I could waste some more time taking it back.

The next day, still gently redolent of Delia Smith's knicker drawer, I decided to buy the wrong sort of antique filing cabinet. But after the footstool debacle my wife said no. So it seemed appropriate that I should develop some kind of illness. This is a good idea when you are at a loose end because everything, up to and including herpes, is better than being bored.

It's hard, I know, to summon up a bout of genital sores at will, but with a little effort you can catch a cold which, if you whimper enough, will easily pass for flu. And yup, even lying in bed watching Judy Finnegan in a Santa suit beats the terminal cancer that is boredom.

Boredom forces you to ring people you haven't seen for eighteen years and halfway through the conversation you remember why you left it so long. Boredom means you start to read not only mail-order catalogues but also the advertising inserts that fall on the floor. Boredom gives you half a mind to get a gun and go berserk in the local shopping centre, and you know where this is going. Eventually, boredom means you will take up golf.

On the day before Christmas Eve I sat next to a chap on the train who, as we pulled out of Paddington, called his wife to say that he was finished, that he had retired and that from now on his life was entirely his own. He was trying to sound happy about it, but there was a faraway, baleful look in his eyes which said it all.

He would spend a month or two at home, breaking interior fixtures and fittings and generally killing everything in the garden, and then one day he would accept an invitation to tee off and that would be it. His life would be over long before he actually stopped breathing. Pity. He seemed like a nice chap.

Or what about fishing? You see those people sitting on the side of the canal in the drizzle and you wonder:

how bored do you have to be at home for that to be better?

The answer, I suspect, is 'not very'. After a week I was at screaming pitch and I couldn't even cook some sausages to put in the fridge because one afternoon, when my wife wasn't looking, I had tried to mend the Aga. And the thing had come off.

I could have put it back, of course, but strangely, when you're not busy, there is never enough time to do anything. I wrote a letter and still have not found enough space in the day to put it in an envelope. Mind you, this might have something to do with the fact that I spent eight hours last Tuesday on the lavatory. Well, it's as good a hobby as any.

Apparently the British work longer hours than anyone else in Europe and stern-faced men are always telling us that this causes stress and heart disease. Fair point; but not working, I assure you, would give us all piles.

Sunday 7 January 2001

All This Health and Safety Talk is Just Killing Me

You may recall that after the Hatfield train crash last year six-chins Prescott, our deputy prime minister, turned up at the scene and gave the distinct impression that with a bit more effort and a lot more investment, nobody would die on the railways ever again.

There was a similar response last week to the news that the number of people caught drinking and driving in the run-up to Christmas rose by 0.1 per cent. All sorts of sandalistas have been on the radio to explain that if the drink-drive limit were lowered to minus eight and the police were empowered to shoot motorists on sight, then death on the road would become a thing of the past.

These people go on to tell us that mobile phones will cook our children's ears, that long-haul flights will fill our legs with thrombosis and that meat is murder. They want an end to all deaths – and it doesn't stop there. They don't even see why anyone should have to suffer from a spot of light bruising.

Every week, as we filmed my television chat show, food would be spilt on the floor, and every week the recording would have to be stopped so it could be swept away. 'What would happen,' said the man from health and safety, 'if a cameraman were to slip over?'

'Well,' I would reply, 'he'd probably have to stand up again.'

Like every big organisation these days, the BBC is obsessed with the wellbeing of those who set foot on its premises. Studios must display warning notices if there is real glass on the set, and the other day I was presented with a booklet explaining how to use a door. I am not kidding.

So you can imagine the problems I shall encounter this week when, for a television series I'm making, I shall climb into a decompression chamber to find out what life would be like on an airliner at 30,000 feet if one of the windows were to break.

The poor producer has been given a form the size of Luxembourg which asks what hazards I will face. Well, my lungs will explode and the air in the cavities under my fillings will expand ninefold, causing untold agony, but I probably won't feel this because there is a good chance that the subsequent hypoxia will turn me into a dribbling vegetable.

I consider it a risk worth taking, but my thoughts are irrelevant because these days my life and how I live it are in the hands of the men from health and safety. The same people who said last year I could not fly in a US-Army helicopter because the pilot was not BBC-approved.

Oh, come on. Everyone knows that American forces are not allowed to crash their helicopters. Following the 1993 debacle in Somalia, when they lost sixteen men who were sent in to rescue two already dead comrades, it has now been decided that no US serviceman will ever be hurt again. Not even in a war.

This has now spread to Britain. You've read, I'm sure, about the hearing damage which can be caused by sergeant-majors who shout at privates, but the plague goes deeper than that. On a visit to RAF Henlow last week, I was rather surprised to see that someone from health and safety had pinned a poster to the notice board, warning the fighter pilots that alcohol will make them aggressive and violent. Oh no, that's the last thing we want – aggressive and violent fighter pilots.

Then we have Britain's fleet of nuclear-powered hunter killer submarines, which have all been grounded or whatever it is you do with boats, by health and safety because they could be dangerous.

Now attention has been focused on Britain's stockpile of uranium-depleted missiles, which are by far and away the best method of penetrating the armour on enemy tanks. Great, except health and safety doesn't like them because it turns out they might kill someone.

Former squaddies are on the news saying that they loosed off a few rounds in Kosovo and now they have caught cancer. Deepest sympathies, but let's look at some facts. They only way depleted uranium can get through the skin is if someone shoots you with a bullet made out of it. It can get into the body through the lungs, but since it is 40 per cent less radioactive than uranium that occurs naturally in the ground, it does seem unlikely that it could cause any damage. I have been down a uranium mine in Western Australia and, so far, I have not grown another head.

However, I do find it odd that the Ministry of Defence will test only soldiers who served in Kosovo and not those who were in the Gulf, where 300 tons of depleted uranium were used and the alpha radiation has had longer to do its stuff. But if by some miracle it does find that our boys have been irradiated and that one squaddie died as a result, then we can be assured that depleted uranium will, in future, be used only on NATO, rather than by NATO.

Where will this end? The US Air Force managed to kill seven British soldiers in the Gulf with what it likes to call friendly fire, so would it not be sensible for those of a health and safety persuasion to ban Americans from the battlefield, too?

Some people say global warming and ozone depletion will kill us. But I'm far more worried about the people who have made it their sworn duty to keep us all alive.

Sunday 14 January 2001

Men are a Lost Cause, and We're Proud of It

Being a man, I am unwilling to pull over and ask someone for directions, because this would imply they are somehow cleverer than me. And obviously they're not, because I'm toasty warm in a car and they're mooching around on foot.

Sometimes, though, and usually in a town where the council has let a group of fourteen-year-olds from one of its special schools design a one-way system, I have been known to give up, become a traitor to my gender and ask a passer-by for advice.

What a complete waste of time. If they begin by saying 'er', then they don't know and you are going to waste hours while they wonder whether you go left at Sketchley's or right. So here's a tip. If someone hesitates when you ask the way, or even if a look of bewilderment befalls their countenance for the briefest moment, drive off.

Of course, some launch immediately into a bunch of militaristic directions, involving clear, concise hand signals and bushy-topped trees at nine o'clock.

But that's of no help either because you won't be listening. It is a known medical fact, and it has been so since the dawn of time, that a man will hear the first word and then shut down.

When the Romans invaded England, they went home to celebrate and didn't come back for 80 years. Why? Because they couldn't find it and, if they did ask for directions in France, they didn't listen.

In the late thirteenth century, Edward Longshanks used women to steer his armies around the realm because they could listen to, and absorb, directions, whereas men couldn't. Actually, I just made that up. But there must be a vestige of truth in it because if he had relied for guidance on his knights, he'd have ended up in Falmouth rather than Falkirk.

Certainly, I didn't listen last week when, having been unable to find the shop I wanted, I found myself drawn inexorably by the man magnet that is Tottenham Court Road into one of those temples to the pagan world of meaningless beeps and unusual hieroglyphics: Computers 'R' Us.

I didn't listen to the voices in my head telling me to get out and nor did I listen when the man started to explain all about a new type of Sony laptop that has too many vowels in its name to be pronounceable. It begins with a V and then you have to make the sort of noise a cat would emit if you fed it through a mangle.

Now don't worry, this isn't going to be a column about how I don't understand computers, and how I wish I were back on the *Rotherham Advertiser* feeding bits of bog roll into a sit-up-and-beg Remington.

I like computers very much and I know enough about them to send emails, write stories and find some ladyboys in Thailand. Unfortunately, however, I do not know as much about them as the people who work or hang around in computer shops, which means my mind does that man thing and stops working.

Like, for instance, if you were offered the choice of Windows 2000 or Windows 98, you'd go for the bigger number. But the man in the shop advised me to spend less on the 98 and, when asked why, proceeded for all I know to talk about his Newfoundland terrier. I did not hear a single thing he said.

The one thing I wanted was an ability to send emails via a cellular phone, so I asked: 'Can I plug this into my mobile?' And he replied . . . but frankly, he may as well have been talking about the problems of making decent onion gravy while marooned in a Nepalese hill fort.

So I ended up buying it . . . and now I think it's broken. Every time I log off from the internet the machine shuts down, casting whatever I've written that day into a silicon no man's land.

Obviously, I could take the computer back to the shop, but then they'll find that I've been looking at ladyboys and this will be embarrassing. Besides, I can't remember where the shop was, and I'm damned if I'm going to ask.

I could phone a friend, but it would be a waste of a call because, as a man, I'm just an ego covered in skin and, if he knows how to solve my problem, that's going to cause some light bruising. So I won't listen. And if he doesn't know, then he's of no help anyway.

At this point, a woman would reach for the instruction book, but this is the single biggest difference between the sexes. Forget the need to be cuddled after sex. And forget spatial awareness and fuzzy logic, because the most butch woman in the world, even Mrs Thatcher, would lie on her stomach for hours with the manual for a new video recorder, ensuring that when she gets back from dinner that night she will have taped the right channel at the right time.

How dull is that. Me? I stab away at various buttons safe in the knowledge that I could be taping something on the other side, next Tuesday, which might be much better.

This certainly helps when playing board games. Because I've never read the rules for Monopoly, I travel around the board in whichever direction seems to be most appropriate, and if anyone says I have to go clock-wise, I respond with a strange faraway look.

It always works. I always win.

Sunday 21 January 2001

We Let Them Get Away with Murder on Radio

It's coming to something when the news is making the news, but that is exactly what happened at the beginning of last week when the papers were full of ITN's victory over the BBC in the Battle of the Ten O'clock Bongs.

The BBC explained afterwards that it had twice as many stories, twice as many live reports and twice as much foreign coverage, but it was stymied by ITV, which ran *Millionaire* two minutes late and went straight to its bulletin without a commercial break.

It even had the gallant knight Sir Trevor McDonald crop up in the middle of Chris Tarrant to say there would be some news soon and not to go away.

This ratings war is getting dirty and deeply annoying. In the past, when programmes largely began on the hour or at half past, you could watch a show on ITV and then, when it had finished, find something else that was just starting on another channel.

But look at the schedules now. Things start at five past and finish at twelve minutes to, so by the time you flick over to the Beeb's new drama series you've missed the explosion and the subsequent car chase and have no idea what's going on.

I understand why it has to happen, of course. When I worked on *Top Gear* it didn't matter whether we were featuring a new Ferrari that ran on water or standing around in a field pretending to be sheep, we always got the same viewing figures. However, if the programme began late, after all the other channels had started their 8.30 p.m. shows, we would drop 1 million or so.

Interestingly, however, this type of 'schedule shuffling' does not seem to be happening in the world of radio.

My wife, for instance, listens only to Radio 4. It could run a two-hour shipping forecast and still she would not retune to another station. I know for a fact that, like the rest of the country, she has no clue what Melvyn Bragg is talking about on *In Our Time*, but every Thursday morning the whole house echoes to the unfathomable pontifications of his stupefyingly dull guests.

At 10.25 a.m. every day I point out that over on Radio 2 Ken Bruce has a good quiz about pop music – a subject she enjoys very much – but for some extraordinary reason she prefers to listen to the state of the sea at Dogger Bank.

I am no better. Left to my own devices I start the day with Terry Wogan, who last week got it into his head that all Chinese people smell of Brussels sprouts. Then it's Ken's pop quiz followed by Jimmy Old.

Now at this point I should turn over, because Old bombards his listeners with the big-band sound and talks to his guests about the price of fish. Then people call up and read out the editorial from the *Daily Telegraph* and it's just not me. But no. I sit there saying that it's only for two hours and then it'll be time for Steve Wright.

Why do I do this? On television I only need to catch the tiniest glimpse of a spangly jacket, the suggestion of a Birmingham accent or the first bar of the *EastEnders* theme tune, and in one fluid movement I reach for the remote and switch over. Yet, displaying the sort of brand loyalty that would cause Marks & Spencer to pickle me in brine, I will drive for hour after hour while Old drones on about how Mrs Nazi of Esher thinks asylum seekers should all be shot.

There is a choice. Obviously Radio 1 is out, unless you enjoy being serenaded by people banging bits of furniture together, and Radio 3 transmits nothing but the sound of small animals being tortured. What about local radio? In London there is Magic FM which broadcasts the Carpenters all day long. Of course, the Carpenters are fine – especially when you have a head-ache – but between the tunes men come on and speak.

I should have thought that being a disc jockey wasn't so bad. I mean, it could be worse. But obviously I'm wrong, because nowhere in the whole of humanity will you find a bunch of people quite so unhappy as the CD spinners on 'Misery' FM.

By 8 a.m. on a Monday they are already counting down the hours to Friday night as though all of us treat the working week as something that has to be endured. In their world, we all work for Cruella De Vil. And it's always raining.

Even if it's a bright sunny day and we've just heard on the news that John Prescott has burst, they would still find something to moan about and then it's on to

Yesterday Once More for the fourteenth time since 6 a.m.

There is no point in going elsewhere because quite the reverse applies. Misery FM is largely run by people on their way down the career ladder, but elsewhere in local radio most of the DJs believe themselves to be on the way up – so they sound as if they're talking to you while someone is pushing Harpic up their nostrils with an electric toothbrush.

'Who knows?' they must be thinking. 'A television producer might be listening, so if I'm really zany and wacky all the time I'll end up on the box.'

Too right, matey, but on television they'll see you coming and switch channels.

On the radio, for some extraordinary reason, they won't.

Sunday 28 January 2001

Willkommen and Achtung,
This is Austrian Hospitality

A small tip. The border between Switzerland and Austria may be marked with nothing more than a small speed hump, and the customs hut may appear to be deserted, but whatever you do, stop. If you don't, your rear-view mirror will fill with armed men in uniform and the stillness of the night will be shattered with searchlights and klaxons.

I'm able to pass on this handy hint because last week, while driving in convoy with my camera crew from St Moritz to Innsbruck, a man suddenly leapt out of his darkened hut and shouted: '*Achtung.*'

I have no idea what '*achtung*' means, except that it usually precedes a bout of gunfire followed by many years of digging tunnels. I therefore pulled over and stopped, unlike the crew, who didn't.

The man, white with rage and venom and fury, demanded my passport and refused to give it back until I had furnished him with details of the people in the other car which had dared to sail past his guard tower.

I'd often wondered how I'd get on in this sort of situation. Would I allow myself to be tortured to save my colleagues? How strong is my will, my playground-learnt bond? How long would I hold out?

About three seconds, I'm ashamed to say. Even

though I have two spare passports, I blabbed like a baby, handing over the crew's names, addresses and mobile phone number.

So they came back, and the driver was manhandled from the car and frogmarched up to the stop sign he'd ignored. His passport was confiscated and then it was noticed that all his camera equipment had not been checked out of Switzerland. We were in trouble.

So we raised our hands, and do you know what? The guard didn't even bat an eyelid. The sight of four English people standing at a border post in the middle of Europe, in the year 2001, with their arms in the air didn't strike him as even remotely odd.

We have become used to a gradual erosion of inter-ference with international travel. You only know when you've gone from France into Belgium, for instance, because the road suddenly goes all bumpy. French cus-toms are normally on strike and their opposite numbers in Belgium are usually hidden behind a mountain of chips with a mayonnaise topping.

But in Austria things are very different. Here you will not find a fatty working out his pension. Our man on the road from St Moritz to Innsbruck was a lean, frontline storm trooper in full camouflage fatigues and he seemed to draw no distinction between the Englander and the Turk or Slav. Nobody, it seems, is welcome in the Austro-Hungarian empire.

The camera crew, who were very disappointed at the way I'd grassed them up and kept referring to me as 'Von Strimmer' or simply 'The Invertebrate', were ordered back to Switzerland. And me? For selling them out, I was allowed to proceed to Innsbruck.

Which does invite a question. How did the guard know where I was going? We had never mentioned our destination and yet he knew. It gets stranger, because minutes later I was pulled over for speeding and even though I had a Zurich-registered car, the policeman addressed me straight away in English.

This puzzled me as I drove on and into the longest tunnel in the world. That was puzzling, too, as it wasn't marked on the map. What's happening on the surface that they don't want us to see?

Finally I arrived at the hotel into which I'd been booked, but a mysterious woman in a full-length evening gown explained menacingly that she had let my room to someone else. And that all the other hotels in Innsbruck were fully booked.

Paranoia set in and took on a chilling air when I learnt that one of the army bobsleigh people I was due to meet the following day had been kicked to death outside a nightclub.

I ended up miles away at a hotel run by a man we shall call 'The Downloader'. 'So, you are an Englisher,' he said, when I checked in. 'There are many good people in England,' he added, with the sort of smile that made me think he might be talking about Harold Shipman.

Something is going on in Austria. They've told the world that the Freedom Party leader has stepped down, but how do we know he's gone and won't be back? Let's not forget these people are past masters at subterfuge.

I mean, they managed to convince the entire planet that Adolf Hitler was a German. Most people here do think Haider will be back. As chancellor. And that's a worry.

I'm writing this now in my room, hoping to send it via email to the *Sunday Times* but each time I try to log on, messages come back to say it's impossible. Maybe that's because The Downloader is up in his attic, looking at unsavoury images of bondage and knives, or maybe it's because I'm being watched. Journalists are.

Either way, I'm nervous about smuggling text like this past customs tomorrow when I'm due to fly home. I shall try to rig up some kind of device using my mobile phone, hoping these words reach you. If they do, yet I mysteriously disappear, for God's sake send help. I'm at the . . .

Sunday 11 February 2001

Gee Whiz Guys, But the White House is Small

If you are the sort of person who gets off on Greek marbles and broken medieval cereal bowls, then there's not much point in visiting an American museum. Think: while Europe was hosting the crusades, the Americans were hunting bison.

However, I have always wanted to see the Bell X-1, the first plane to travel faster than the speed of sound, so last weekend I set out for the Smithsonian Institute in Washington, DC. The trip was not a complete success because the X-1 was swathed in bubble wrap and housed in a part of the museum that was closed for renovation. But never mind, I found something else.

There are those who think America is as richly diverse as Europe – they're hopelessly wrong, and Washington, DC is the worst of it. I'd never realised that it isn't actually in a state. The founding fathers felt that, if it were, the others would feel left out – and that's very noble. Except it means that residents of the capital city of the free world have no vote.

Another feature it shares with Havana and Beijing is the immense sense of civic pomposity. The downtown area is full of vast, faceless buildings set in enormous open spaces and guarded by impossibly blond secret-service agents in massive Chevy Suburbans. The pavements are marble and the policemen gleam.

Just three blocks south of Capitol Hill you find yourself in an area where 70 per cent of the population are gunmen and the other 30 per cent have been shot. Then to the west you have the dotcom zone, which is full of idiotic companies with stupid names and unintelligible mission statements. Half.formed.thought.corp: Bringing the World Closer Together.

You look at those huge mirrored office blocks and you think: 'What are you all doing in there?' The politicians will never have the answer as they all live in an area called Georgetown, which is as antiseptic and isolated from the real world as the sub-basement at a centre for research into tropical diseases.

Here, the only cannon is Pachelbel's. It was nice to find it playing in the lobby of my hotel. It made me feel safe and cosseted, but it was on in the lift and in the bookstore next door, and in the art gallery.

It was even playing in the 'authentic' Vietnamese restaurant where customers can gorge themselves on caramelised pork in a white wine jus. Now look, I've been to Saigon and in one notable restaurant I was offered 'carp soaked in fat' and 'chicken torn into pieces'. A difficult choice, so I went for the 'rather burnt rice land slug'. I have no idea what it was, but it sure as hell wasn't caramelised or served in a wine sauce.

Still, what do the Americans know about Vietnam? Well, more than they know about France, that's for sure. The next morning I ordered an 'authentic French-style country breakfast' which consisted of eggs sunny-side up, sausage links, bacon, hash browns and – here it comes – a croissant. Oh, that's all right then.

What's not all right are the people who were eating there. Every single one of them was a politician, or a politician's lapdog, or a political commentator or a political lobbyist.

Because all these people with a common interest live together in a little cocoon, they labour under the misapprehension that their work is in some way important. They begin to believe that there are only two types of people: not black or white, not rich or poor, not American or better; just Democrat or Republican.

So what, you may be wondering, is wrong with that? Surely it's a good idea to put all the politicians together in one place, it saves the rest of us from having to look at them.

I'm not so sure. When Peter Mandelson couldn't remember whether he'd made a phone call or not he had to resign and it was treated as the most important event in world history. On the television news a man with widescreen ears explained that Tony Blair might actually delay the election, as though everyone, in every pub in the land, was talking of nothing else.

That was London. But in a town built by politicians for politicians, it's much, much worse. You can't even build a skyscraper in Washington, DC, because all buildings must be smaller than the Washington Memorial. The message is simple. Nothing here is bigger than politics.

To explain that there's a world outside their window, and it's a world of dread and fear, I felt compelled to buy some spray paint and a ladder and write something appropriate in big red letters on the White House.

But when I got there I simply couldn't believe my eyes. Put simply, I live in a bigger gaff than the president of America, and that's not bragging because, chances are, you do too. It really is pathetically small.

All around there were television reporters revealing to their viewers some snippet of useless information that they had picked up the night before over a bowl of authentic Ethiopian pasta. And I wanted to say: 'Look, stick to what's important. Tell everyone that President Bush lives in a hut and, most of all, warn people that the X-1 display at the Smithsonian is closed.'

Sunday 18 February 2001

Flying Round the World, No Seat is First Class

According to recent scare stories, people on the 27-hour flight to New Zealand have a simple choice. You can either die of deep vein thrombosis or you can die of cancer which is caused by radiation in the upper atmosphere reacting with the aluminium skin of the aeroplane. Both options are better than surviving.

I boarded the plane at Heathrow and was horrified to note that I was to share my section of the cabin with a couple of dozen pensioners on a Saga holiday. Great. Half were at the stage where they'd need to go to the lavatory every fifteen minutes, and half were at the stage where they didn't bother with the lavatory at all.

But the seat next to me was free. So who am I going to get? Please God, not the girl with the baby I'd seen in the departure lounge. There is nothing worse than sitting next to a girl with a baby on a long-haul flight. I got the girl with the baby.

And then I was upgraded to first class. I didn't stop to ask why. I just took the moment by the bottom of its trouser leg, moved to the front and settled down with my book. It was a big fattie called *Ice Station*, which promised to be the sort of page-turning rollercoaster that would turn the fat 11-hour leg to Los Angeles into a dainty little ankle.

Sadly, it turned out to be the worst book ever written. Just after the lone American marine had wiped out an entire French division single-handed, I decided to watch a movie instead. But since I'd seen them all, in their original formats, with swearing, I was stuck.

You can't even talk to the stewardesses because they think you're trying to chat them up and you can't talk to the stewards either, for much the same reason. So I thought I'd get a drink, but of what?

My body clock said it was time for tea but I'd already moved my watch and that said I should have a glass of wine. But I couldn't have a wine because then I'd want a cigarette and you can't do that on a plane because, unlike a screaming baby, it's considered antisocial.

I know. I'll look out of the window. I'll look at this overcrowded world in which we're living. Well sorry, but for six hours there are no towns, no people and despite various claims to the contrary no evidence of global warming. Just thousands upon thousands of miles of ice.

So I went back to my book and was halfway through the bit where the lone American was busy killing everyone in the SAS, when we dropped out of the clouds and into Los Angeles.

Time for a smoke. But this being California, that meant I had to go outside, which meant I'd have to clear customs, which meant I had to get in line with the Saga louts who'd all filled their forms in wrong.

I queued for an hour while the American passport-control people, in a bad mood because work stops them eating, barked at the old biddies and then realised that time was up. Unlike everywhere else in the world, airlines in the States are allowed to take off with your bags on board.

And so with a heavy heart and even heavier lungs I trudged back to the 747 for the next, really long leg and found that my first-class seat had gone. But then so had the girl with the baby.

In her place there was a Californian beach babe who was going to Auckland with her equally volleyballish friend.

To begin with, I didn't think too much of the fact they were holding hands but as the flight wore on and they started holding rather more intimate parts of one another's bodies, the penny dropped.

I know I shouldn't have been surprised. I've been told countless times that people are born gay and that it's not something that happens because you're too much of a boiler to pull a bloke. So there must be good-looking lesbians, too. It's just that, outside films, you never see one.

I tried to read my book, in which the hero was now taking on and beating the entire US Marine Corps using nothing but a rope ladder, but it was impossible to concentrate. And you try sleeping when you're seventeen inches from two pneumatic blondes playing tonsil hockey.

Somewhere around the Fiji islands they went to sleep, and so did I, waking up an hour later when I moved my arm and the nicotine patch tore a couple of armpit hairs clean out of their sockets.

After twelve hours we landed and I had forty minutes to make my connection for Wellington which, even though the domestic terminal is a brisk fortnight's walk away, was just about doable, providing all went well in customs.

It didn't. A man took my papers into a back room and emerged ten minutes later wearing rubber gloves. I damn nearly fainted.

Believe me, you do not want an intimate body search after a 27-hour journey. You don't want an intimate body search after a 27-minute journey, come to think of it, but thankfully he limited his probing to my suitcase and I made the last flight with one minute to spare.

On it, I had another breakfast, finished my godawful book and tomorrow, after just 36 hours in Wellington, I'm coming home again. This is jet-set living? You can keep it.

Sunday 25 February 2001

They're Trying to Lower the Pulse of Real Life

Did anyone else notice that, in the aftermath of last week's train crash, the newspapers were gripped with a sense of impotent rage? Try as they might, and some of them tried very hard indeed, they couldn't find anyone to blame.

The tracks hadn't disintegrated. The train driver wasn't four. There were crash barriers on the motorway bridge and the man in the Land Rover hadn't fallen asleep. It had been an accident.

But, of course, there's no such thing as an accident these days. If you trip over a paving stone or eat a dodgy piece of meat, there will be an inquiry, someone will be culpable, and steps will be taken to ensure it doesn't happen again.

We had a very wet autumn, as I'm sure you will recall, and as a result many rivers burst their banks. But this was not an act of God or a freak of nature. This was someone's fault.

Nobody is allowed to just die, either. George Carman QC, for instance, pegged out at the age of 71, which is not a bad innings. But oh no. His death has been chalked up to cancer, as though it might have been avoided if he'd not eaten cheese and broccoli.

Well now look. The human being, and the human

male in particular, is programmed to take risks. Had our ancestors spent their days sitting around in caves, not daring to go outside, we'd still be there now.

Sure, we're more civilised these days, what with our microwave ovens and our jet liners, but we're still cavemen at heart. We still crave the rush of adrenaline, the endorphin highs and the buzz of a dopamine hit. And the only way we can unlock this medicine chest is by taking a risk.

Telling us that speed kills and asking us to slow down is a bit like asking us to ignore gravity. We don't drive fast because we're in a hurry; we drive fast because it pushes the arousal buttons, makes us feel alive, makes us feel human.

Dr Peter Marsh, from the Social Issues Research Centre in Oxford, says the recent rise in popularity of bungee jumping, parachuting and other extreme sports is simply man's reaction to the safer, cotton-woolly society that's being created.

He told me this week that, when the youth of Blackbird Leys in Oxford was stealing cars and doing handbrake turns back in the 1990s, a number of liberal commentators called to ask him why.

'It's funny,' he said. 'These kids steal a really good car, take it back to their housing estate and charge around, with all their friends cheering and applauding. They are having a laugh, and making the police look like fools on television, and you have to ask why!'

Who has decided that we must live in a temperance

society where there is no stimulation, no risk, no danger and no death?

In the past two months alone we've been told that water makes us mental, that coffee increases the risk of miscarriage, that lawn mowers cause deafness and that middle-aged men who dance will get 'glamrock shoulder'.

A professor at Aberdeen University described washing-up bowls as 'an absolute menace'. We were told that snooker chalk causes lead poisoning and that the new euro coins contain nickel, which will blister skin. There were warnings too that apples cause *E-coli* and that mercury thermometers kill babies.

So where is all this rubbish coming from? Well, to be honest, it's being imported from America, where scientists are now worried that a consignment of Play-Stations that has been sent to Iraq could be linked to form a crude supercomputer. This, they say, could then be used to pilot a chemical warhead all the way to Buffalo Springs.

Americans, remember, have got it into their heads that you can now wage a war without losing a single soldier or airman, and we see the same sort of thing with their weather too.

Instead of shrugging when a hurricane marches across Florida, or a tornado tears up Oklahoma, they insist that the government does something about it. They want more warning, better protection.

Then of course there is the business of smoking.

Did you know that there are now porno websites in America where you can call up pictures of girls with farmyard animals, and then, at the highest level, for members only, pictures of fully clothed girls enjoying a cigarette?

And despite a few plaintive cries for help from the back of the *Washington Post*, the public over there seems to have bought into this belief that life can, and should, be run without risk, that all accidents are avoidable, and that death is something that only happens to people who eat meat and smoke.

This is odd. From the outside, Americans appear to be human – a little larger than normal, perhaps – but equipped nevertheless with arms and heads.

So how come they are able to overcome the base instincts that drive the rest of mankind?

I can think of only one answer. If they do not need risk and stimulation, they must be genetically malformed. There's a simpler word for this. They must be mad.

Sunday 4 March 2001

Forget the Euro, Just Give Us a Single Socket

If you were charged with the task of standardising an entire continent, from the Baltic to the Bosporus, I'm pretty sure you would come up with a list of things that are slightly more pressing and important than a single currency.

Plug sockets, for a kick-off. How can it be that our MEPs have managed to homogenise a banana, yet they still allow each member state to offer a new and exciting way of getting electricity out of the wall?

This wasn't so bad when we travelled with only a comb, but now that we need to charge up the batteries in our computers, mobile telephones and electronic organisers it means we must pack a vast array of adaptors; so many in fact that you now need to travel like an E. M. Forster heroine, with fourteen trunks and Cummerbund Akimbo, your manservant.

And then the check-in girl has the temerity to ask if your bags contain any electrical appliances. Damn right they do.

This is deeply maddening for me since I have always prided myself on being able to survive abroad for up to a month on nothing but hand luggage. I have even developed a routine whereby one pair of underpants can be made to last for four days.

You wear them back to front on day two, inside out on day three and then inside out and back to front on day four. I know a cameraman who claims to have developed a combination that allows a five-day switch-over routine, but frankly I don't believe him.

Then we have telephone connections, which in the past were of no great importance. But now we all have internets, how come there is no edict from Brussels on what is, and what is not, a standard socket?

They launch the euro, which means I won't need a wallet that bulges with different currencies. Big deal. Yet they're happy to have me stomping around the Continent with enough cable in my suitcases to build a suspension bridge.

It's also very difficult with road signs. Only the other day, while searching Zurich for the A3 motorway to St Moritz, a blue sign said turn left and a green sign said turn right. Blue is motorway, yes? Nope. Not in Switzerland it isn't. The blue sign takes you on the sort of road that made the cabling in my suitcase look straight.

And lifts: why can't there be a standard letter that denotes the reception level? It has been agreed that all across Europe prisoners have an inalienable right not to fall over and yet it is deemed acceptable for people like me to spend hours stabbing away at meaningless buttons and emerging half a day later in the hotel boiler room.

Now I don't want you to think that I long for the days when newspapers ran headlines saying 'Fog in the Channel. Europe cut off'. I don't subscribe to the British-is-best mentality, because we have John Prescott and fuss and mutt. We have much to learn from the Continent.

Austrian lavatories, for instance, are plainly a good idea. There's a short flush for your number ones and a full-on Niagara for even the most stubborn number two. Then you have three-hour lunches in Spain and smoking bars on long-haul French airliners.

So, surely, if we must have European integration, it should be a case of taking the best bits that each country has to offer and blending them into the other member states.

Take customs officers. In Germany you get poked in the chest by a hippie with a gun, and woe betide anyone who tries to get a carnet signed in France. I tried this last week and the man at the desk couldn't be bothered. He so couldn't be bothered that, when pressed, he hurled the form across his office, shouted '*merde*' at nobody in particular and stomped off.

I want to see an implementation of the system they have in Italy, i.e. no system at all.

It might be useful, too, if we could find a universal butt for European wit. We have the Irish, the Swedes have the Norwegians, the Dutch have the Belgians and so on. What we need is a universal whipping boy so that jokes translate smoothly.

No, not the Welsh. At dinner last week in Austria, there were sixteen people round the table and, really, it was like a bunch of flowers. There were Scandinavians, Germans, Brits, Italians, the lot, and it was great.

We explained the jokes for the Germans, the French

chose the wine, the Italians ordered the food, the Austrians talked to the waitress and the Dutchman spent his evening stopping the Swede from trying to commit suicide. We laughed at one another, joked with one another, learnt from one another and it was just the most perfect evening; a shining example of European cooperation and harmony.

It was spolit by only one thing. There, in the middle of our arrangement of roses, bougainvillea, edelweiss and tulips, complaining that we smoked and doing mock coughs to hammer the point home was a giant redwood: an American. He did not understand Wiener schnitzel and couldn't grasp the notion that we would want another round of drinks.

Sure, he was the perfect butt for all of us, but we must remember that he comes from a federal superstate where the plug sockets are all the same. It's a worry.

Sunday 18 March 2001

I'd Have Laid Down My Life for Wotsisname

The court case involving Jonathan Woodgate threw up an interesting dilemma last week when his best friend gave evidence against him. So what do you do?

On the one hand, society cannot function without honesty, so therefore you know it's right to offer your services to the prosecution. But then again, friendship is supposed to be an unshakeable bond which cannot exist without loyalty. So it is also right that you should keep shtum.

Well, I thought about this long and hard in the shower this morning and I've decided I'd squeal like a baby. Because you know something? Friendship is not an unshakeable bond at all. It's like a gigantic sand dune, seemingly huge and permanent, but one day you get up and it's gone.

Back in the early eighties I spent pretty well every Saturday night with the same group of friends in a King's Road basement bar called Kennedy's. We laughed all the time, we went on stage with the band, we sang, we drank ourselves daft and we knew, with the sure-fire certainty that night will follow day, that we'd be mates for ever.

Had one of them been accused of gouging the barman's eyes out with a lawnmower, I'd have told the police I was dead at the time and that I knew nothing. I would even have taken the heat on his behalf, had push come to shove. Which would have made me feel awfully foolish today because I have no idea where two of those friends are, and, for the life of me, I cannot even remember what the third one was called.

How did this happen? Presumably, when I said good-bye for the last time ever, I really did believe I'd be seeing them all again the following weekend. It wasn't like we'd had a row, or that they'd all grown beards or moved to Kathmandu. We just went home and never saw one another again.

And this happens all the time. I went through my address book earlier and there are countless hundreds of people, friends, muckers, soul mates and former colleagues who I never ever see.

Here's the problem. What I like doing most of all in the evenings, these days, is sitting in a gormless stupor in front of the television, eating chocolate.

Going out means getting up, getting changed, finding a babysitter, arguing about who'll drive and missing *Holby City*. And quite frankly, that's not something I'm prepared to do more than once a week. So, the most people I can hope to see in a year is 52, which means it would take two years to see everyone in my Filofax.

Except, of course, it would take much longer than that in reality because people who I'm not seeing on purpose endlessly invite me round for dinner until eventually I've used every excuse in the book, up to and including being attacked by a Bengal tiger, and I have to go.

And then, as the day in question dawns, I mooch around the house, dreaming up the amount I'd pay to someone if they came through the door and offered me a guilt-free get-out-of-jail card. Once I got up to £25,000, but still no one came, I had to go and, as a result, another week went by without seeing Mark Whiting, a friend from my days on the *Rotherham Advertiser*.

And, of course, the more time that goes by, the harder it becomes to call on people who you haven't seen in ages. I mean, if someone you haven't heard from in ten years suddenly telephones, you know full well that it'll be for one of two reasons. He has lost his job. Or he has lost his wife.

I have become so desperate about this friends business that I recently asked my wife not to put any new people in the address book. I don't care how nice they are. I don't care if he is funny or that she's allergic to underwear. We have now got enough friends.

This went down badly and so we've reached an agreement. New people can only go in the book providing old ones are Tipp-Exed out.

This is not easy. There's one bloke called (name and address withheld because I'm weak) who I really don't want to see again. Given the choice of people I'd call to ask for a night out, he'd come below the woman in the video-rental shop.

Worse. If I saw him coming down the street towards me, I'd pretend to be gay and lunge endlessly for his genitals until he went away. And if that didn't work, I'd run into the nearest butcher's and feed myself into the bacon slicer.

But even so, as I stood there with the Tipp-Ex hovering above this crashing bore's name, I could hear his voice in my head, and it sounded like Hal in *2001: A Space Odyssey*. 'Don't do it, Dave. Remember all those nights we shared, Dave. I'll try to be more interesting next time, Dave.'

I couldn't do it and so now I've got a much more radical solution, pinched from anyone who's ever tried to get out of a love affair with someone they don't really love any more. I need him to ditch me.

So what I shall do, first thing in the morning, is take a leaf out of the Leeds United book on friendship, call the police, and shop him for that joint I saw him smoke back in 1979.

Sunday 15 March 2001

Creeping Suburbia isn't Quite What I Expected

You may be surprised to hear that the two words most feared by those who live in the countryside are not 'foot' and 'mouth'. Or 'mad' and 'cow'. Or even 'Blair' and 'Prescott'. No, out here the most terrifying words in the English language are 'Bryant' and 'Barratt'.

If the cows in our paddocks were to develop sores or a fondness for line dancing, we'd simply set fire to them. But this option would not be available should one of the big development companies plonk a dirty great housing estate at the end of our garden. And tempting though it may seem, we couldn't call in the armed forces, either.

'Hello. Is that the RAF? Oh good. I'd like to call in a napalm airstrike, please, at these coordinates.'

When a housing estate comes to your little world you are stuffed. Your views are ruined, your house becomes worthless and you needn't expect much in the way of sympathy or compensation from His Tonyness.

Quite the reverse in fact, because unlike the spread of foot-and-mouth, which is being driven by the wind, the plague of housing developments is actually being driven by Tony, who's said that over the next six minutes the countryside needs another 30 million bungalows.

I went last week to exactly the sort of place that Tony has in mind. It's a nearly completed development called

Cambourne Village and it is to be found in the flatlands of Cambridgeshire between Royston and Norway.

It's big. So big that it's been built by a consortium of all the big developers. There's a business park, a high street, a pub that does the sort of food that is garnished with garnish, three village greens, a lake and a helmetless teenage boy who rides around the network of roads all day on an unsilenced motorbike.

They've even tried to crack religion. Obviously, the vast majority of people who'll come to live in Cambourne will be white, middle class and Church of England. But, of course, in these days of multiculturalism you can't just stick up one church and be done with it. So, to cope with that, the single church will be multidenominational.

Quite how this will work in practice, I have no idea. Maybe there's an inflatable minaret round the back somewhere. Maybe they hang up the tapestries when the Catholics are in, and then it's all whitewashed when the lone Methodist from No. 32 fancies having a bit of a sing-song.

I was thinking that this kind of thing might lead to jealousy, and maybe even a small war. But then I thought of something else. If there's going to be any backbiting in Cambourne, it'll be over who gets what house.

You see, unlike any estate I've ever seen, every single property in the whole damn place – and there are more than 3,000 of them – is different. Large, £260,000, double-fronted village houses with PVC sash windows and garages nestle right next door to small two-bedroom cottages which, in turn, are jammed up against three-bed semis, some of which plainly have ensuite bathrooms and some of which don't.

This looked like an anthropologist's worst nightmare. 'Not only does the man at 27 have a wooden, Sussex-style garage for his BMW 318i but he also has a 20 × 20 lawn, with a tree. And if you stand on the avocado bidet in his back bathroom, he has a view of the lake!'

Sounds like a hideous way to live until you remember that all proper villages are like this. There's a manor house, a dower house, a smithy, a home farm, some tied cottages, a council estate and a boy on a motorbike. It's normal. What's not normal are the housing estates of old, where every single property is exactly the same as all the others. And everyone has a BMW 318i.

That is what's wrong with Milton Keynes. Yes, you never sit in a traffic jam and yes, there's always somewhere to park. But all the houses are the same. They appear to have been pushed out of a Hercules transport plane and parachuted into position.

In Cambourne, it's all different. And some of it is very, very pretty. There's one row that put me in mind of Honfleur in Normandy. And as I wandered around, I started to feel little pangs of jealousy.

I thought I had it all worked out, living in the middle of the Cotswolds, but I have no neighbours to chat to and there are no other children to keep mine amused. In Cambourne you can walk to the shops, walk to the pub, walk to church and walk to work. I could walk for two days and I'd end up with nothing more than muddy shoes.

They've even got their own website, where residents can sell bicycles and share wife-swapping tips.

And they don't even have to put up with the usual drawbacks of village life like an annual bus service, tractors and men in jumpers deafening all and sundry with their penchant for campanology. Though I would imagine that when the inflatable minaret is pumped up, things might get a bit noisy.

But you know the absolute best thing about Cambourne? It's not in Oxfordshire. Which means it's not in my back yard. It's in Cambridgeshire. Which means it's in Jeffrey Archer's.

Sunday 1 April 2001

Is It a Plane? No, It's a Flying Vegetable

So, the Bubbles have cancelled their order for 60 Euro-fighter jets, saying they need the money to pay for the Olympic Games. Well, thanks Mr Popolopolos.

That's just great.

Eurofighter could, and should, have been a shining example of pan-European cooperation. One in the eye for Uncle Sam. The greatest ground-attack 'mud mover' the world had ever seen. But instead it will stand for ever more as a beacon, showing the world that a federal superstate can never work on this side of the Atlantic.

The idea for such a plane was first hatched back in the early 1970s when Britain realised it would soon need a land-based fighter bomber to replace both the Jaguar and the Harrier. We couldn't design such a machine by ourselves because we were on a three-day week at the time, so we went to see the French and the Germans.

The French said they already had a fighter, the Mirage, and therefore only needed a bomber which could be used on aircraft carriers. The Germans said they didn't need a bomber since, for once, they weren't planning on bombing anyone. They needed a fighter. And they absolutely were not interested in this aircraft-carrier business because they didn't have any.

Obviously the whole thing was never going to work,

so in the spirit of what was to come the three countries did the sensible thing, signed a deal and went back home to come up with some preliminary studies.

Now, to understand the hopelessness of the position I would like you to imagine that they were not designing a warplane but a vegetable. So Britain came up with the potato, France designed a stick of celery, and Germany did a lobster thermidor. The project was dead.

But not for long. From nowhere, the Italians and Spanish suddenly decided that they wanted a piece of the action and, flushed with the idea of these extra complications, a new contract was drawn up.

It was ever so straightforward. The amount of work, and therefore jobs, given to each country would depend on how many of the fighters they would buy. That was fair. But not to the French it wasn't. They wanted one plane, 50 per cent of all the work and total control, and when they were told to get lost, they did.

Taking Spain with them.

So now it was Britain, Germany and Italy and it stayed that way for about twelve seconds, when the Spanish fell out with the French and asked to come back in again. So fifteen years after the project was first mooted and just eighteen months before the RAF needed its planes, the project at last was up and running.

Then disaster. The Berlin Wall fell over and all of a sudden European governments lost the will to spend trillions on a plane that would have nobody to fight. The air forces, too, realised that a highly manoeuvrable, Mach-2, dogfighting jet would have no place in the new world order. So it was agreed by everyone to keep going.

Germany and Britain were going to take 250 Euro-fighters each, which is why we each had 33 per cent of the workload. But in the recession of 1992 our governments wondered if this was a trifle excessive. The RAF dropped its order to 232 planes and the Luftwaffe to just 140. But the German government insisted that it kept its share of the work. When everyone else kicked up a fuss it threatened to pull out.

Fearful that the pack of cards was about to come tumbling down, the Italians and Spanish went to lunch and the British got tough. Immediately, we gave in to the Germans.

However, the delay had thrown up a new problem: the name. All along it had been called Eurofighter 2000, but by 1994 it was obvious that it could never be operational until 2001 at the earliest. So it became the Typhoon, which conjures up pictures of devastation and death.

Well, don't get your hopes up. You see, Tony Blair recently decided that the plane's missiles should be British rather than American. Good call, but the British weaponry won't be available until eight years after the jet goes into service. So what are the pilots supposed to do in the meantime: make rude gestures?

That said, though, I have talked to various authoritative sources over the past year and it is widely thought that Eurofighter will become the world's best fighter-bomber. It is desperately easy to fly and at £50 million a pop it is also extremely cheap. To put that in perspective, each new USAF F-22 Raptor will cost £115 million.

So Eurofighter is something about which Europe can be justifiably proud. Should the Russians ever decide to invade, we will have exactly the right sort of fire power to hold them back.

However, for dealing with sundry world leaders in far-flung parts of the globe, what you really need are aircraft carriers. Britain has just ordered two and there was talk of modifying Eurofighter to become precisely what the French wanted 30 years ago. But presumably it was too much of an effort. So what have we done? Well, in a perfect spirit of European cooperation, we have teamed up with the Americans to build something called the Joint Strike Fighter. Thank you, Europe, and goodnight.

Sunday 8 April 2001

Is This a Winner's Dinner or a Dog's Breakfast?

No. I mean, yes. Yes, I have just been to Barbados but no, I didn't stay at Winner Central, the newly reopened Sandy Lane hotel. Why? Because I checked, and for bed and breakfast only, a fortnight there for a family of five would cost £44,000.

So, who's going to fork out that kind of money for two clean sheets and a croissant? Not David Sainsbury, that's for sure. He was staying in our hotel down the road. And not the TetraPak Rausings, either. They were holed up in their bungalow.

Obviously, I had to find out and since you can't just walk in for a nosey, I had to bite the bullet and book a table for dinner. So I called to make a booking and was told that if I didn't turn up, $100 would be deducted from my credit card. Christ. A hundred bucks for not going.

When you arrive you are shown by the doorman to a woman at the reception desk who shows you to a man who shows you to the door of the restaurant, where a man shows you to the man who shows you to your chair. I felt like the baton in a relay race.

Or rather I would have done but sadly I was still at the gate, in the back of a taxi being stared at by a guard with a piece of curly flex connecting his ear to the back of his jacket. He probably thought it made him look like an FBI agent, but in fact it just made him look deaf. Which is why I resorted to shouting at him.

I was told subsequently that it is poor form to turn up in a taxi and that I should really have arrived in a proper car. Which would have meant buying one. And that would have been even more expensive than turning round and going home. I hadn't really gone to the Sandy Lane for the food. I'd gone to see the people. So you can imagine the crushing disappointment of finding that the restaurant was not a sparkling sea of *Cheshire Life* gold shoes, with a sprinkling of noisy New Yorkers. In fact, only two other tables were occupied.

To my right there was Bewildered Dotcom Man, who'd gone to bed one night, a struggling geek on 38p a year, and woken up the next morning to find he was worth $4 billion. He was wearing a short-sleeved Hawaiian shirt, see-through white trousers and was accompanied by his wife, Janet.

To my left there was White Tuxedo Man. He was with his wife, Sylvia, to whom he uttered not one word. He spent most of the evening either reading the credit cards in his Filofax or talking into his mobile phone . . . which would have been impressive except that I have the absolute latest Ericsson, which works on Everest, in the Mariana Trench and even in Fulham. But it couldn't get a signal in Barbados, so sorry, sunshine, you weren't fooling anyone.

So, with no other guests to laugh at, we thought we'd have a giggle at the food. Good idea, but I couldn't find it.

It turned out that there was a sliver of what looked like corned beef on my plate, but it was so thin that when you tapped it with a knife it made a clinking noise. I tried scooping it up with a fork, and then a spoon, but neither was successful, so in the end I gave up and just licked the plate. What did it taste like? Well, meat, I guess, with a porcelain afterglow.

Then the water came. There had been an enormous song and dance with the wine but this was just a dress rehearsal for the main event. The waiter unscrewed the cap as though defusing a nuclear bomb and for one glorious moment I thought he was going to ask me to sniff it.

But that would have been only mildly ridiculous. So instead, he poured a splash into the glass for me to taste. 'No, really. Unless you got it out of Michael Winner's bath, just pour away. It'll be fine.'

Drinking at the Sandy Lane, though, is nothing compared to what happens when you need to expel it. In the lavatory you are offered a choice of bog roll – plain or embossed. And that is just so Wilmslow.

Before leaving we were given a ballot paper on which we were asked to vote for the evening's 'champion', the waiter who'd impressed us most. The losers, presumably, are lobbed into the shark pool.

And then we got the bill, which was the funniest thing of all because, when translated into English, it came to £220. The lobster-salad starter, all on its own, had been £32, and for that I'd have expected the damn thing to get up and do a song and dance routine. Instead, it had just sat there, being a dead crustacean. A bit like White Tuxedo Man's wife.

I don't care what you read over the coming weeks by hacks on freebies, the Sandy Lane is preposterous. If you were given all the money in the world and told to design the most stupid restaurant on the planet, you wouldn't even get close. I mean, you wouldn't think to put the waiters in pink trousers, would you? They have, though. And pink shirts.

But that said, it is a good thing. Every resort should have a place like this, a giant black hole that hoovers up precisely the sort of people that the rest of us want to avoid. Once you know they're there, you can go somewhere else.

Sunday 29 April 2001

Call This a Riot? It was a Complete Washout

Following the success of last year's anti-beefburger riot when protesters gave Winston Churchill an amusing Mohican haircut and planted cannabis seeds in Parliament Square I was rather looking forward to last week's rematch. Obviously I was a little concerned that my car might be turned over and burnt, so I booked a chauffeur-driven Mercedes and spent the day hunting what Jack Straw had promised would be a festival of rubber bullets and Molotov cocktails.

Secretly, I was hoping for some water-cannon action. There is something really funny about the sight of an angry young woman being hosed into the gutter by a tank. If Jimmy Savile could be coaxed out of retirement, this would be top of my *Fix It* hit list: the chance to propel a vegetarian into the middle of next week.

I was also hoping that at some point I could sneak off and lob a brick through Pringle's window on Regent Street. Just because.

But London was as quiet as the grave. All morning we cruised the streets and all we saw was a man in a kaftan posing for photographers at Marble Arch. And, like every other shop in town, Pringle had boarded-up windows.

Eventually we found the mob and I would like to

bet that if I gave you 2,000 guesses, you'd never guess where they were. What symbol of capitalism had drawn them to its portals: Nike Town, McDonald's, the American Embassy? Nope. They were outside New Zealand House.

Except they weren't. I counted 17 television crews, well over 100 reporters and photographers, 75 policemen and . . . 14 protesters.

Disappointed, I went for lunch at the Ivy hoping that something would kick off in the afternoon. But it didn't. I heard on the radio that Regent Street was closed and so, keen to see if Pringle was under attack, I hurried over there to find 2,000 policemen dressed up as navy seals surrounding two women who were so angry about something or other that they had decided to sit down in the middle of the road.

Unbelievable. The police had rented every van in Europe, there was a helicopter chewing fuel in the sky and why? Because two women were cross about men, or student loans, or East Timor or whatever it is that angers women at university these days.

So what's the problem here? How come every other city in the world staged a pretty good riot and all we got was a brace of lesbians – and I quote from radio reports – 'throwing paper at the police'?

To understand why the British are so hopeless at getting off their backsides, we need to go back to the summer of 1381 and the so-called Peasants' Revolt. A mob, seeking equality for all, had sacked London. They had burnt the houses of the rich, beheaded anyone dressed in velvet, opened prisons, drunk John of Gaunt's wine and scattered financial records to the four winds. These guys were on a roll. The army had fled, the king, Richard II, was just fourteen years old and his bodyguards were so scared they had gone into hiding. Then the mayor of London compounded the problem by sticking his dagger into the neck of the protesters' leader, Wat Tyler.

Now you would think, wouldn't you, that this would inflame the situation somewhat. (If Ken Livingstone had stabbed one of the lesbians, the other would have become incandescent with rage.) But no. Ten days later, the rebels confronted the king who told them: 'You wretches, detestable on land and sea; you who seek equality with lords are unworthy to live.' So they all went home.

How come? What was it that extinguished the fire in their bellies? Well, I have no proof of this because nobody was keeping meteorological records in the four-teenth century but I'd like to bet that it started to rain.

A lot of people with vast foreheads have, over the years, wondered why Britain has never had a successful uprising. Some say it's because the monarchy was too powerful. Others argue that you can't have a revolution if you have a strong and contented middle class.

Pah. I say it's because of the drizzle. Last year's May Day riot was a success because it was dry and quite warm. This one was a washout because it rained and we are brought up on a diet of party invitations that always say 'If wet, in the village hall'. And you can't change the fabric of society from a venue that's also used for parish council meetings and line dancing.

There is some evidence to back up this theory. The night of 11 April 1981 was dry and unseasonably warm. I know this because it was my twenty-first birthday. It was also the night of the Brixton riots. Then there was Toxteth and it wasn't raining on the television coverage of that, either.

Aha, you might say, but what about the Russian Revolution? They also have rubbish weather so how did they get it together? Well, look at the dates. It began in early spring and it was all over by October. And when did the French storm the Bastille? It was 14 July.

Here's a thought: the only reason why the Arabs and Jews have managed to keep their nasty little war going for 50 years is because it never bloody rains. If the post-war powers had put Israel in Manchester, there'd have been no bloodshed at all.

Sunday 6 May 2001

Being a Millionaire is Just One Step from being Skint

So, the other night, I was sitting around after dinner playing the board game of *Who Wants to be a Millionaire?* with Hans and Eva Rausing.

At first, I was slightly bothered that they didn't seem terribly interested in getting the questions right but then, of course, it struck me. As builders of the TetraPak fortune, becoming a millionaire means taking a significant step backwards.

It made me laugh. And then it made me think. Even if we leave billionaires out of the equation, who does want to be a millionaire these days? I mean, £1 million is just enough to ensure that you lose all your friends but not quite enough to buy anything worthwhile.

You see those poor souls with Chris Tarrant, shuffling up to the centre of the stage with their shirts not tucked in and their dreadful shoes, saying that, if they won the big prize, they'd buy an island and move there with Meg Ryan. No you wouldn't. A million doesn't even get you a decent flat in Manchester these days and, even if it did, you're not going to pull Meg Ryan with it.

The simple facts of the matter are these. Fifty new millionaires are created in this country every day. When American Express launched its plutocratic black card, the initial print run of 10,000 was snapped up in days.

According to the Inland Revenue, more than 3,000 people earned more than £1 million last year, which means there are now 100,000 people across the country who have a million or more in liquid assets.

But if you include people whose houses or shares in companies are worth more than seven figures, then you arrive at an alarming conclusion. There are probably half a million millionaires in Britain.

So why, then, can you hear yourself think this morning? Why is the sky not full to overflowing with Learjets and helicopters? How come your dog is not cowering under the table in case someone tries to turn it into a coat? Why isn't everyone married to Meg Ryan? Why does Pizza Express not offer a panda-ear and tiger-tail topping?

These days, to live what we still perceive to be a millionaire lifestyle, you need to have a damn sight more than £1 million.

How much more, though, that's the question. Back in 1961 Viv Nicholson won £152,000 on the pools and promptly embarked on a pink and furry spending spree, commensurate with what in today's money would be £3 million. And it lasted precisely fifteen years before she went broke.

A recent report said that, to live the super-rich lifestyle today, with a personal stylist to do your hair and a fast, convertible car to mess it up again, you actually need £5 million, but I'm not sure that this is going to keep you in pointy shoes and Prada.

I mean, Mr Blair is going to help himself to 40 per

cent, leaving you with £3 million, which becomes £2.5 million once you've set aside a little something for school fees.

You then buy the big house in the country, and that leaves you with liquid assets of £1 million, which sounds great. But hang on a minute: you're part of the so-called super-rich now, so you can forget about holidaying at CenterParcs. You're going to be taking the family and the nanny, in the front of the aeroplane, to the Caribbean every year.

Lovely, but do that for twenty years at £50,000 a pop and you'll get home one day to find a letter from the bank manager saying he is 'disappointed to note that you have no money left'.

All you'll have to show for your £5 million is a suntan, a terraced house and surly children who would rather have gone to the local comp.

I suspect that to live a boat-filled, choppery existence off Venice one minute and St Kitts the next, you actually need £10 million. But then, if you have this much, if your bank balance is bigger than your account number, you're going to spend every night for the rest of your life at charity auctions being expected to stick your hand up and buy the big lot: the signed Frankie Dettori underpants.

Every day you'll be approached by people who either need backing for their new publishing venture in Azerbaijan or an operation for their not-very-ill six-year-old niece.

Oh sure, other very rich people will ask you to come

and stay at their Tuscan villas but, when you get there, you'll have to share a breakfast table with a man who runs guns for the Iranians, a woman with an Argentine accent who's permanently bored and a gaggle of airheads who throw you in the pool.

You'll ricochet from pillar to post, a one-man social-services department until, one day, your wife shacks up with the under-gardener and you end up alone in the Savoy, knowing that all the friends you used to have are sharing a bottle of Bulgarian plonk in a Chiswick pizza joint, laughing a lot and carefully splitting the bill afterwards.

I therefore have a new idea for a television game show. It's called *Who Doesn't Want to be a Millionaire Any More?* All the contestants are super-rich and the idea is to give away as much money as possible in the shortest time.

The trouble is, of course, that nobody would phone the hotline. They'd all be at home with their lovely wife Meg, admiring their signed Frankie pants.

Sunday 13 May 2001

What Does It Take to Get a Decent Meal Round Here?

At this time of year *Country Life* magazine swells as its property pages fill to overflowing with six-bedroom manor houses, each of which can be bought for the price of a stamp.

You may be tempted by the notion of a crunchy gravel drive and a selection of stone mushrooms, but before taking the plunge look carefully at the photograph of the 'far-reaching view'. There's nothing in it, is there? Just fields, foxes and a millstone grit outcrop on the far horizon.

It may appear to be pleasant and tranquil but it's going to be a big problem when you're looking for a restaurant. You see, fields do not eat out. Millstone grit outcrops are not to be found demanding a glass of Sauternes to wash down the pudding. Foxes don't like cappuccino.

On Tuesday my wife and I were celebrating eight years of perfect wedded bliss and thought it would be fun to toast the moment with a simple but expensive dinner somewhere posh.

Le Manoir aux Quat' Saisons is not too far away but frankly it may as well be on the moon because we're not going again. Why? The last time we went it was hosting a convention for photocopying engineers who spoilt the evening somewhat by making me pose for photographs with their cars.

No matter. There used to be a great restaurant in Oxford called the Lemon Tree, but now it has new owners who said that if we wished to smoke, we would have to sit in a special raised area. This sounded a bit like a naughty chair. So that was out.

The Petit Blanc was crossed off the list next because, oddly, it only allows smoking at weekends. Owner Ray White should be advised that people who smoke do so because they have to. It's not like fishing. Tell someone they can't go to the canal until Saturday and they'll be fine, whereas smokers won't. They'll start eating your tablecloths, and if you object, you'll be on the receiving end of what I now believe is known as 'a Prescott'.

After an hour on the phone it looked like we'd have to give up and eat in a pub which, as I'm sure you know, is slightly less appealing than eating the pub itself. The only thing I can say about 'pub grub' is that it tastes like I cooked it. And I am the only person in the world who can make cauliflower taste like the back of a fridge freezer.

Eventually, we found a rather nice smoker-friendly fish restaurant called Dexters in Deddington, which is a local place for local people, all of whom were not celebrating their wedding anniversaries, or indeed anything. That's why they were at home and we were the only people in there.

So, one has to presume, it will eventually close or ban

smoking and then that'll be it. We'll have to start eating the millstone grit outcrops.

I'm not kidding. I live in the Cotswolds, one of the most affluent, sought-after areas in the whole country – a six-bedroom manor house round here costs more than a whole book of stamps – and yet there is only one worthwhile restaurant within a half-hour's drive. One. And it's empty.

However, before everyone in London splits in half with mirth I should point out that the three worst meals I've ever eaten were all at well-known restaurants in Notting Hill. Last week.

In one we were told by a waiter, who looked like his house had just burnt down, that the chef had messed up the food and that most of it was off. We never saw the wine we ordered, my crab starter was covered in wallpaper paste and after two hours the main course still hadn't turned up at all.

And I'm not alone. Everyone I've talked to recently is saying that their favourite restaurant is starting to deliver what tastes like hamster droppings to table 9 at 10 p.m., when it should have gone to table 14 at 7 p.m.

But this was inevitable because while the countryside has no restaurants at all, London has far too many. Take West End Lane in Hampstead. It used to be a shopping street but all they can offer now, apart from a hair-cut and a bijou flat for the price of Gloucestershire, is a plate of spaghetti that should have gone to table 8 last week.

A year ago the situation was so bad that restaurateurs were reduced to trawling Paris for waiting staff. Some reports suggested that as many as 10,000 surly, off-hand Pierres had migrated to London. And that was then.

Now, with more and more new restaurants opening every day, I'm surprised Marco Pierre White isn't to be found at the traffic lights offering jobs to passing motorists. Hell, I'm surprised he isn't offering them to the Albanian window washers.

You see, it's all very well employing the best chef in the world, but what's the point if you can't find someone to take it from the kitchen to the dining room? Well, someone with a sense of direction and a basic grasp of English anyway.

I was disappointed the other day when my six-year-old daughter said she wanted to be a waitress when she grew up. The way things are going she could get a job now. Unfortunately though, there aren't any openings round here. Indeed, the only place where you can get a decent steak is called a pyre.

Sunday 20 May 2001

Cutting Lawns is the Last Word in Civilisation

Having seen *Emmanuelle* in Bangkok, I thought I knew what a massage would be like. Well it isn't.

The first disappointment comes when you find that there will only be one masseuse, and the second when you discover that his name is Bill.

Then things really start to go pear-shaped. After asking you to undress and lie face-down on the bed, he'll tell you that you're tense. And you'll want to reply that this is not surprising because you were not expecting someone who learnt all about body pressure points while serving as a Spetsnaz assassin. But all you'll manage is a muffled 'Aaaaaaaargh'.

Be assured, a proper massage gives you some idea of what it would be like to fall down a mountain while locked in a fridge freezer. It would be more relaxing to have your fingernails torn out while being force-fed with used engine oil.

I have discovered that the best way of soothing away the stresses and strains of the working week is to mow the lawn. Sitting there, with the sun on your back, concentrating on nothing but going in a straight line and not running over the flowers, you can actually feel your muscles turning to jelly and your teeth unclenching.

And then, when you've finished, you can stand back

with your hands on your hips and admire the sheer geometric perfection of that verdant test card, that subtle blend of absolute straightness in a curved and wild world. You have taken on nature and, with nothing more than a Honda Lawnmaster, brought civilisation and order to the unruly forces of nature. Well done. You are now a lawn bore.

You will start shouting at your children if they ride their bicycles on your immaculate conception. You will tut when you find discarded cigarette butts. You will stand for hours in the garden centre eying up trowels, and you will talk about Roundup with your friends in the pub.

I am now such a lawn bore that when I discovered a thistle that had dared to show its hideous, ugly face in my perfect turf I shot it.

And while I like having a fighter plane in the garden − it's better than a water feature because the children can't drown in it − I was inconsolable when I saw the damage that had been done while it was being towed into position. There were three grooves, each a foot deep, stretching all the way from the broken electric gates to my dead yew hedge.

This, you see, is my problem. I want to be a gardener. I want a potting shed and some secateurs. I want *Homes & Gardens* magazine to profile my work, but all I can do is cut grass. Everything else turns to disaster.

Two years ago the field across the road was planted with saplings and I bought precisely the same stuff for a patch of land next to my paddock. Today, his trees are 12–14 feet tall. Mine have been eaten by hares.

I filled the grooves in the lawn with ten tons of the finest topsoil money can buy and then, to speed the repair along, mixed some grass seed with the most expensive organic compost in the world and sprinkled it all on top. And the result? Three long and unsightly strips of mushrooms.

I was assured that my yew trees would grow at the rate of a foot every twelve months but they did nothing of the sort. For the first two years they just sat there and then they decided to die. So they did.

So I was intrigued last week by the fierce debate that appeared to have been raging at the Chelsea Flower Show.

There are those who like gardens to be traditional, a Technicolor riot of flora and fauna harmonised to create a little piece of harmonised chaos. These people are called gardeners.

Then you have the modernists who think it is much better to throw away the plants and replace them with stark concrete walls and gravel. These people are called Darren and you see them every week on *Ground Force*.

The Darren philosophy is tempting. First of all, you get a quick fix, a well-planned and attractive garden in a couple of hours. And second, the whole thing can be maintained by taking the Hoover to it once a year.

But these modern gardens do feel a bit like rooms without roofs, and you will lose things in the gaps of your decking. I know one man who lost his wife down there.

So what about the gardening option? Well, all things considered, it doesn't sound quite so good. I mean, what's the point of planting an oak tree when the best that can happen is that it stops being a twig just in time for the birth of your great-great-great-grandson. And the worst is that it commits suicide.

Furthermore, if you go down the gardening route, you will have to spend your entire retirement in crap clothes with your head between your ankles. You will then get a bad back and that will require terrifying and undignified weekly appointments with Bill at the massage parlour.

So what's the answer then? Well, I've just bought an acre or so and I'm going to employ the third way. I'm going to do absolutely nothing, and next year I shall call it 'the New Labour wilderness', and transport it to Chelsea where it will win a gold medal.

Sunday 27 May 2001

An Invitation from My Wife I Wish I Could Refuse

What would life be like if parties had never been invented? Tents would still be used solely as places for Boy Scouts to sleep, there would be no such thing as a plate clip and you would never have heard an amateur speech.

There would be no black tie, no parking in paddocks, no chance of running into former spouses and you would never have drunk a warm Martini, garnished with ash, at four in the morning because the rest of the booze had run out.

We're not even programmed to enjoy parties that much. Think. When you were little you liked your teddy and you liked your mum, but other children were the enemy. You were forced to go, and sat on your bottom waiting to be humiliated by someone saying: 'Oh dear. Who's had a little accident then?'

You always have little accidents at parties. No sooner are you out of nappies than you're straight into the flowerbed where the hostess's mother finds you face down at dawn. And then when you're married, you get in huge trouble for dancing with the wrong girl in the wrong way for too long.

I mention all this because three weeks ago I caught the perfect illness. There was no pain, just an overwhelming need to lie in bed all day eating comfort food and watching *Battle of the Bulge*.

I was enjoying myself very much, but halfway through the afternoon my wife tired of popping upstairs with trays of quails' eggs and mushroom soup and, with that hands-on-hips way that wives have when their husbands are not very ill, announced that I should get up and organise a party for her fortieth birthday. 'You have 21 days.'

My first chance to have a little accident came with the invitations. Every morning we get invites but we have no idea who they are from or where the party is being held because the typeface is a meaningless collection of squirls, and all the instructions at the bottom are in French. RSVP.

I thought the solution would be simple. Write in block capitals and use English. But oh no. Nowadays, it's important to make your invitation stand out on the mantelpiece, so it must be written on an ingot or a CD-Rom or on a man's naked bottom.

The printer was quite taken aback when I asked for card. 'Card?' he said. 'Gosh, that really is unusual.' And then he gave me an estimate: 'For 150 invites, sir, that will be £6.2 million. Or you could go down to Prontaprint and have exactly the same thing for 12p.' Right.

The next problem is deciding on a dress code. What you're supposed to do these days is dream up a snappy phrase such as 'Dress to thrill' or 'Urban gothic', but since none of our friends would have the first clue what any of this meant, I put 'No corduroy'.

With just two weeks to go I called a party organiser to help out with the event itself. 'All we want,' I explained, 'is a bit of canvas to keep the wind off everyone's vol-au-vents.'

Well, it doesn't work out like that because he sits you down and says that you really ought to have some kind of flooring. It's only £170. So you say fine. And then he says that electricity might be a good idea, too. It's only £170. Everything is only £170, so you end up ordering the lot.

When the estimate came, I really was ill. 'What would you like?' asked my wife, seeing that this time I wasn't faking. 'Some fish fingers? A nourishing bowl of chicken soup? *Where Eagles Dare*?' No. What I want is for everyone we've invited to come over all dead.

It was not to be. With a week to go, only six had had the decency to say no and the next day, two changed their minds.

Except, of course, we hadn't heard a whisper from anyone who has ever appeared on television. It is a known fact that once you've been on the electric fishtank, even if it's just for a moment in a Dixons shop window, you lose the ability to reply to party invitations.

So you've got the caterers asking how many they should cook for and you're having to say they'd better get Jesus in the kitchen because it could be five or it could be five thousand.

Then the guests start telephoning asking what they should wear instead of corduroy and where they can stay. Here's a tip. When you're looking for a hotel in

Chipping Norton, you're more likely to find out what's good and what's not by calling someone in Glasgow. People who live in Chipping Norton usually have no need of local hotels. And I don't care what you wear. And yes, your ex-husband will be here. And no, I'm not going to tow you out of the paddock if it turns into a quagmire.

You'll probably have a miserable time but look at it this way. It'll be much more miserable for me, and even more miserable for the poor old dear who lives next door. As the band wheeled in their speaker stacks, I called her to explain that there might be a bit of noise on Saturday night. 'Oh I don't mind,' she said. 'What is it? A dinner dance?'

No, not really, it's more a chance for all my wife's wildly disparate groups of friends to come and not get on with each other.

Sunday 10 June 2001

How Big a Mistake are *You* Going to Make?

Many years ago, when I was working as a local news-paper reporter, the editor sent me to cover the inquest of a miner who'd been squashed by an underground train.

Hours into the interminable proceedings a solicitor acting for the National Coal Board told the court that the deceased 'could' have stood in an alcove as the train passed. And I wrote this down in my crummy shorthand.

But unfortunately, when I came to write the story, I failed to transcribe the meaningless hieroglyphics properly. So what actually appeared in the paper was that the man 'should' have stood in an alcove as the train passed.

Well, there was hell to pay. Damages were handed over. A prominent apology was run. The lawyer in question shouted at me. The family of the dead man shouted at me. The editor shouted at me. The proprietor shouted at me. I was given a formal written warning about my slapdash attitude. And here I am, twenty years later, with my own column in the *Sunday Times*.

We hear similar stories from the City all the time. Some trader, dazzled by the stripes on his shirt, presses the wrong button on his keyboard and the stock market loses 10 per cent of its value. He gets a roasting and later in the year spends his seven-figure bonus on a six-bedroom house in Oxfordshire.

So I feel desperately sorry for the Heathrow air traffic controller who was found last week to be guilty of negligence when he tried to land a British Airways 747 on top of a British Midland Airbus. He has been demoted and sent in eternal shame to wave table tennis bats at light aircraft in the Orkneys.

The problem here is that we all make mistakes, but the result of these mistakes varies drastically depending on the environment in which we make them.

When a supermarket checkout girl incorrectly identifies a piece of broccoli as cabbage and you are over-charged by 15p, nobody really cares.

But what about the man who incorrectly identified a live bullet as blank, put it into the magazine of an SA-80 army rifle and heard later that a seventeen-year-old Royal Marine had been killed as a result?

The inquest last week recorded a verdict of accidental death and now the dead soldier's father is said to be considering a private prosecution and a civil action against the people responsible for his son's death. I don't blame him, of course. I would do the same. But the fact remains that as mistakes go, loading the wrong bullets into a magazine is exactly the same as loading the wrong information about broccoli into a checkout weighing machine.

Think about the chap who was employed by P&O ferries to shut the front doors on the car ferry *Herald of Free Enterprise*. I have no doubt that he performed his badly paid, noisy, repetitive and unpleasant job with the utmost diligence until one day, for reasons that are not clear, he forgot.

Now if he had been a warehouseman who forgot to shut the factory gates when he left for the night, there may well have been a burglary. And that may well have put a dent in the insurance company's profit and loss account. But he wasn't a warehouseman and, as a result of his momentary lapse, water rushed into the car deck and 90 seconds later the ship was on its side. And 193 people were dead.

He was not drunk at the time. He did not leave the doors open to see what would happen. He just fell asleep.

So what's to be done? Well, you can employ the Health and Safety Executive to dream up the most fool-proof system in the world, the sort of money-no-object set-up that I'm sure is employed at Heathrow. But the fact remains that all systems rely on human integrity to some extent and, if someone takes their eye off the ball for a moment, two jets with 500 people on board can get within 100 feet of one another.

Or you could argue that people who hold the lives of others in their hands should be paid accordingly. But I don't think the size of a person's bank balance affects their ability to concentrate. I mean, His Tonyness is on £163,000 a year and he makes mistakes all the time.

No. I'm afraid that fairly soon we are going to have to accept that a blame culture does not work. We are going to have to accept that doctors, no matter how much training you give them, will continue to stick needles into people's eyes, rather than their bottoms. We are going to have to accept that, once in a while, Land Rovers will crash onto railway lines causing trains to crash into one another. We are going to have to stop penalising people for making that most human of gestures – a mistake.

And the best way of doing this is to ban those 'Injured at work?' advertisements for solicitors on the backs of buses.

So long as there's an opportunity to profit from the simple, unintentional mistakes of others, then there will always be a desire to do so. To lash out. To blame. To turn some poor unfortunate soul who just happened to be in the wrong job on the wrong day into a human punchbag.

Sunday 17 June 2001

America, Twinned with the Fatherland

Europe offers the discerning traveller a rich and varied tapestry of alternatives. You may go salmon fishing in Iceland or sailing off Greece. You may get down and dirty on the French Riviera or high as a kite in Amsterdam. You can bop till you drop in Ibiza or cop a shop in London. And we haven't even got to Italy yet.

So why then do a significant number of Americans, having decided to take that vacation of a lifetime over here, always start the tour in Germany? Because Germany is to holidays what Delia Smith is to spot welding. Perhaps it's because they've heard of it. Maybe they have a brother stationed at Wiesbaden or perhaps their father did some night flying over Hamburg back in 1941. Yes, I know that's before America joined the war, but judging by the movie *Pearl Harbor*, they don't.

Or maybe in the brochures Germany somehow looks appealing to an American. I mean, both peoples tend to eat a little more than they should and both have a fondness for driving very large automobiles, extremely badly. Both countries also have absolutely hopeless television programmes where the hosts dress up in vivid jackets and shout meaningless instructions at the contestants. An American flicking through the 215 one-size-fits-all alternatives in his Stuttgart hotel room would feel right at home. Until he got to Channel 216, after midnight, and found a whole new use for a dog.

Both countries enjoy the same British exports, too: Benny Hill, Mr Bean, Burberry mackintoshes. Then there's the question of taste. Only two countries in the world would dream of teaming a tangerine bathroom suite with purple and brown carpets. And only two countries go around pretending to be democracies while burdening the people who live there with enough regulations and red tape to strangle everyone in China. Twice. In Germany, you must not brake for small dogs and you must have a licence before you can play golf. An American would nod sagely at that.

So, it would appear that Germany and America are identical twins and now you may be nodding sagely, remembering that some 25 per cent of Americans are derived from German stock. Indeed, shortly after Independence, there was a vote in the Senate on whether the official language of the fledgling USA should be English or German.

Whatever, a great many Americans spend vacation time in the Fatherland, including, just last week, a retired couple from Michigan called Wilbur and Myrtle. They packed their warm-weather gear into a selection of those suitcases that appear to be made from old office carpets, got their daughter Donna to drive them from the gated community they call home to Detroit airport, where they flew for their holiday to Cologne.

Myrtle had packed some powdered milk because she'd caught a report about foot-and-mouth disease in

Europe and figured she'd better stay safe. Wilbur was worried about catching KGB from beef that had been infected with BSM and vowed on the plane he'd stick to chicken. Both wondered if you could get chicken in Europe.

I know this because I know the man who lent them a car. They liked him very much, not simply because he spoke such good English but also because, contrary to what they'd heard, he could stand on his hind legs. Myrtle asked whether they should go to Munich because an antiques fair was in town or if it was better to visit Frankfurt which, she'd heard, was the Venice of Germany. 'Well,' explained my friend, 'there is a river in Frankfurt but it's probably stretching things a little to think of it in the same terms as Venice.'

Still undecided, they set off, and that should have been that. But just two hours later they were on the phone. It seems that they'd become a little confused and strayed into Holland, where they'd found a charming little café that did chicken.

Unfortunately, however, while they were inside someone had broken the back window of their car and helped themselves to all their belongings: not only the Huguenot felt-tile suitcases but also their passports, driving licences and Wilbur's wallet.

Maybe the thief was a drug addict after his next fix. Or maybe he'd mistaken them for Germans and had taken everything in exchange for the theft of his father's bicycle. Or perhaps he'd taken umbrage at their registration plate. All Cologne-registered cars this year begin with KUT, which is Dutch for the worst word in the world.

Either way, poor old Wilbur and Myrtle were not having much luck with the police, either in Holland or Germany, to which they'd returned. They decided after just six hours in Europe that they'd had enough and were going to fly home. So they did.

The problem is, of course, that while Germany may superficially have some things in common with America, it is not even remotely similar once you go beneath the surface. There's no 'have a nice day' culture in Germany. The German does not care if you have a nice day because he is a European.

I'm writing this now in a town called Zittau on the Polish border. I feel at home here.

Sunday 24 June 2001

Cornered by a German Mob Bent on Revenge

So there I was, cruising into town with the top down when, with the crackle of freshly lit kindling, my map hoisted itself out of the passenger side footwell and, having spent a moment wrapped round my face, blew away.

Ordinarily this would not be a problem. I had the name of a bar where I could watch the Grand Prix and I even had its address. So I would simply pull over and ask someone for directions.

Unfortunately, I was in Germany where, if someone doesn't know exactly what you are looking for, they won't tell you at all. To make matters worse, I was in the eastern part of the country where there are no people to ask anyway.

I first noticed the problem in the achingly beautiful Saxony town of Zittau which, at 8.30 on a Friday night, was deserted. It was like a scene from *On the Beach*. Further up the autobahn in the city of Zwickow, *Aida* was playing at the opera house but there were no queues. The shops were full of expensive cutlery sets but there were no shoppers. There were car parks but no cars.

The latest figures suggest that since the Berlin Wall came down, some towns have seen 65 per cent of the population migrate to the west in search of work. I do not believe this. If 65 per cent have gone, then 35 per cent must still be there. Which begs the question: where the bloody hell are they?

West Germans are paying a special 7 per cent tax at the moment for a new infrastructure in the east. Chancellor Kohl promised this would last for three years but twelve years have elapsed and still the spending goes on.

A recently leaked report from Wolfgang Thierse, the German parliamentary speaker, painted an apocalyptic picture of the east as a region on the verge of total collapse. We think we have problems with migration from the north of England to the south-east but ours are small fry and we are not hampered by having the lowest birth rate in the world.

In the year before unification 220,000 babies were born in East Germany. Last year just 79,000 births were recorded.

They are pumping billions into the former GDR so that everything over there is either freshly restored or new. The lavatories flush with a Niagara vigour. Your mobile phone works everywhere. The roads are as smooth as a computer screen. But it's like buying a new suit for someone who is dead.

And that brings me back to Sonderhausen on that boiling Sunday, when I had twenty minutes to find the bar before the German Grand Prix began.

With nothing but the sun for guidance, I just made it and in my rush failed to notice that the bar was located in the worst place in the world. It was a quadrangle of jerry-built communism; a faceless ten-storey, four-sided slab of misery and desolation. And there, in the middle of it all, was the Osterthal Gastshalle.

I have drunk at roughneck bars in Flint, Michigan, and Kalgoorlie in Western Australia. I am no stranger to the sort of places where the optics are rusty and the chairs are weapons. But the Osterthal was something else. The only light came from a brewery sign above the bar and a fruit machine in the corner. But this was enough to note that there were eight people in there, none of whom had any teeth.

But, I said to myself, this is okay. This is a mining town. I'm from a mining town. I know that in mining towns you don't ask for a glass of chilled Chablis. So I ordered a beer and settled back to watch the race.

It did not last long. Pretty soon one of the toothless wonders sauntered over and offered the international hand of friendship. A cigarette. Except it wasn't a cigarette. It was called a Cabinet and it was like smoking liquid fire. 'Is good yah?' said the man, helping himself to fistfuls of my Marlboros.

Then things grew a little serious. Could I, he asked, explain what was written on the television screen? It's just that despite the much-vaunted school system in the old GDR, he couldn't read. But he could speak English, providing we stuck to old Doors lyrics.

Have you ever tried this: commentating on a motor race using nothing but the words of Jim Morrison? It's difficult. 'Heinz-Harald Frentzen. This is the end. You'll never look into his eyes again.' By lap 50 I was struggling badly and, to make matters worse, they had each consumed 150 litres of beer and were ready for a good fight.

Ordinarily, I guess, they would ram each other's heads into the fruit machine but today they had a much better target: me, the western git. A living, breathing example of the faceless capitalistic machine that had moved into their town, bought the mine, asset-stripped it and shut it down.

They had lost their jobs, the free kindergarten places for their children and most of their friends. In exchange they had got a new sewage system. Now I was facing a simple choice: watch the end of the race or get my head kicked in.

What these people want, more than anything, is to have the Berlin Wall back. What I want, more than anything, is to know who won the Grand Prix.

Sunday 1 July 2001

Wising Up to the EU After My Tu

Ordinarily I don't talk about the European Union. But when you are in Brussels, the capital of Belgium and the capital of Europe, it's hard to stay off the subject for long.

Yesterday I settled down in an agreeable square with a charming and erudite Irish girl who has lived here for four years. We spent four seconds on the prettiness of Bruges, eleven seconds talking about Jean-Claude Van Damme and then I could contain myself no longer.

'What exactly,' I demanded brusquely, 'has the EU done for me?'

I'm sorry, but the night before I had arrived at the Presidents Hotel behind two coachloads of tourists who could neither read nor understand the fantastically enquiring registration cards. It's interesting, isn't it: you don't need a passport to enter Belgium, but you do need a passport number before they will let you stay the night.

Still, it was only a small wait of two hours before I was issued with a key to what was basically a double-bedded blast furnace. Immediately, I knew this hotel was designed and run entirely for the benefit of visiting Americans, a people who seem unable to cope unless a room is either hot enough to boil a fox or cold enough to freeze nitrogen.

a.m. I had dragged my pillow into the minibar
was trying desperately to get some sleep when the
man next door decided what he'd like to do most of all
was to play squash. So he did. For about an hour.

Having worked up a sweat, he then decided that what
he needed was a nice long shower. So he did that for an
hour, too. Then he figured it would be a good time to
call the folks back home in Iowa. Although why he used
the phone I am not entirely sure.

'Hey Todd,' he yelled, 'it's Chuck. Listen how loud
I can make my TV go.' I haven't had the chance to
check yet but I feel fairly sure that if you look in *The
Guinness Book of Records* to see who has the loudest voice
in the world, you will find it's good old Chuck. And
boy, does he have a lot of friends. So many that by the
time he had finished calling them all, it was time for
another game of squash. Eventually, I had to call reception to ask if they would ring the man and ask him to
go to sleep. I heard him pick up the phone.

'Hello,' he bellowed. 'Yeah, sure.' Then he put the
phone down, knocked on my door and whispered at the
sort of level that can splinter wood: 'Sorry, buddy.' Then
the sun rose and in the same way that it always seems to
find the crack between the sun visors in your car, it
found the crack in my curtains and bored a line of pure,
superheated radiation straight into my left retina, so I
had to get out of the minibar and back into the Aga that
was my bed.

Understandably then, the next day I was not in the
mood for small talk about Jean-Claude Van bloody

Damme. 'Come on,' I persisted. 'What has the EU ever done for me?'

My companion, a fervent Europhile, explained that she would not have been able to go to an Irish university because she had been educated in England and, as a result, could not speak Irish. 'Well,' I said, 'that's very wonderful but how does it help me?'

She had to agree it didn't but, unfazed, went on to explain that because of the EU leather shoes must now sport an EU-approved symbol showing they are made of leather.

Hmmm. I'm not sure that this, on its own, is quite enough to justify the two-centre, three-tier government with its staff of 35,000 people, especially as most of us are clever enough to recognise the difference between something that came from the bottom of a cow and something that came from the bottom of a Saudi oil well. 'No,' I said. 'This leather thing is going nowhere. You must do better.'

She told me that because of the EU designer clothes were now cheaper in the UK, but since I'm not big on Prada I don't care. Then she said that were it not for the council of ministers there would be more air pollution. Wrong subject, I'm afraid. Twenty minutes later, after I had finished explaining precisely how little damage is being done to the world by man and his machines, she moved on.

Apparently, if I go to a country where no British embassy is operating (neither of us could think of one) and got myself arrested for drug smuggling, I could call for help from any EU member state which was operating a mission there.

So, if you get banged up in Kabul for producing heroin – and this, believe me, is very unlikely – and it turns out that the Foreign Office has been forced out for some reason, you can go to the Swedes.

And that, after an hour of soul-searching, was all she could come up with. Cheap, bureaucratic leather shoes and help from the Vikings if things go pear-shaped in some Third World hellhole.

That night I checked into a hotel where the chambermaids were hosting a 24-hour Hoover race. My room was on a tricky little corner where most of them crashed into the skirting board.

This, I suspect, is why the EU doesn't really work. None of the people who run it is getting any sleep.

Sunday 8 July 2001

A Weekend in Paris, the City of Daylight Robbery

Last Sunday a Connex Third World commuter train broke down, due to the wrong type of government, just outside Sevenoaks in Kent. This forced both inbound and outbound Eurostar trains onto a single track, causing delays of up to five hours.

Predictably, the passengers were said to be 'disgusted'. Those in cattle class said that all they'd been offered was a free glass of water, while those in first class said they couldn't get any sleep because the carriage doors made too much noise.

It all sounds very grim. And very strange. Because I was on one of the trains and I never even noticed there was a problem. Sure, we left Waterloo at a brisk saunter and rattled past Sevenoaks at a stately crawl but this is what I'd been expecting. Time and again we are told that Eurostar doesn't work and that the tunnel is full of rabies and German tanks.

That's why I've always chosen to go to Paris in a car, in a plane, on a boat; on my hands and knees if necessary. Anything rather than the train which could give me a disease and catch fire 20,000 feet beneath Dogger Bank.

However, let's just stop and think for a moment. It is never reported that every motorist driving to Paris is stopped by the constabulary and made to stand naked in a freezing cell while they raid his pension plan to pay for the inevitable speeding fine. Nor do you ever read about flights being diverted to Bournemouth due to the wrong type of air.

This happened to me last autumn. My car was at Gatwick. I had landed at Hurn. So what did I do? Get on a train and go straight to London, or get on a bus for a three-hour trip round the M25 so I could be reunited with my wheels? The answer, as far as I know, is still parked at Gatwick in car park G, row 5.

The result is that last Sunday I chose to go to Paris on Eurostar. The first-class ticket cost me FFr2,000 so it's more expensive than flying. But from the centre of London to the centre of Paris it is ten minutes faster than going in a Boeing.

You can smoke, too, so who cares that the carriage doors open as though they've been blown apart with Semtex and that the clanky drinks trolleys have square wheels?

However, I'm not sure that Paris was the right destination. It's funny, isn't it, that Haussmann's low-rise, starburst city of lurve is always first choice for a romantic weekend break and yet, when you stand back for a moment, you have to wonder why.

Obviously, the metropolitan pomp is extraordinary and the whole place does give good fountain, but in recent years it has become dirty, down-at-heel, more rude than ever and yet somehow less interesting. On the dark and broody Left Bank, left-wing Jean-Paul Sartre types have been driven away by high rents and the aristocracy has retired to its clubs on Rue St Honoré.

You are left with a vast and chewy middle class and at this time of year even that is busy sunning itself on the beaches of Biarritz. Paris is therefore like the elephant house without the elephants. It's bereft of anything. Except perhaps a sense of menace; a sense that, really, you should put your wallet down the front of your underpants.

It's not as bad as Detroit, obviously, where you wouldn't get 30 yards before someone put a hole in your head so they might steal your toenails. Or Puerto Rico where the hotel guards said it would be best if I stayed at the bar. But it's bad all right. At night, Paris has eyes.

Carjacking, for so long the preserve of Muscovite gangsters and urban Durbanites, is now an everyday occurrence. Elsewhere in Europe the weapons of the needy are a sponge and a bucket of water, but at the traffic lights in France it's a pistol and an instruction to get out.

The French, displaying a Latin leaning to the right, blame immigration, saying Paris was fine before it was swamped with half of Macedonia. But the fact is that I felt tempted to steal something the first time I sat down at a pavement café and ordered a couple of beers.

This was in Montparnasse, which is nothing special, and yet the bill was ruinously preposterous. I paid ten bleeding quid for two poxy 1664s and half a dozen olives. Then there was my laundry bill in the hotel: £180. It would have been cheaper to buy a washing machine.

And we haven't even got to the food which, I was assured, would restore my faith. Even the worst-looking dive, they said, would conjure up a taste sensation. Everyone in France, apparently, is born to cook.

No, they're not. The first time I ate out I was struck, for the first time ever, with loose stool syndrome; the second, my lobster had been nuked (they probably got it from Mururoa atoll); and the third, I got a plate of what tasted like a smoked inner tube.

So, all I can say is that if you're looking for a dirty weekend of rumpy pumpy, forget Paris. They'll nick your condoms. And make you eat them later. At £500 a pop.

What I would do is get on the train and do what you always want to do on the plane – turn left. That way, you'll end up in Bruges where you can walk round quite safely in a hat made of money, gorge yourself silly on pig's trotter sausage and have a very, very nice time.

Sunday 15 July 2001

It's a Work of Art, and It was Built on Our Backs

I suppose that in the world of jet travel we have all seen some noteworthy modern architecture. The arch at La Défense in Paris. The new Reichstag building in Berlin. The Transamerica Tower in San Francisco. And yes, even the Millennium Dome.

But no matter what you've seen or where you've been, the Guggenheim Museum in Bilbao is enough to blow your underwear clean into next week. Some say this vast, curling edifice resembles a ship; others say it's a big steel fish; while those of an architectural bent argue that it echoes Bilbao's maritime past while drawing on the town's more recent flirtation with heavy industry.

The truth, however, is that it sits in the city like the Taj Mahal would sit in Barnsley, dominating the sightlines and your thought processes with equal aplomb. It's there at the end of every street, and when it isn't it's etched on your mind.

You can be halfway through a bowl of paella half a mile away and you are drawn, as if by some invisible force, to get up from your table for yet another look. It's the aurora borealis. It's a moonlight rainbow. It's a meteor shower and a tornado and the most magnificent African sunset all rolled into one. It is the most amazing thing I have ever seen. And I have seen Kristin Scott Thomas in the nude. So, obviously, I had to go inside.

On the top floor was an exhibition of frocks by Giorgio Armani which, I'm told, was a runaway success when it was shown at the Guggenheim in New York recently. This, of course, means nothing because Americans will turn up in great numbers to watch a tractor move.

Unfortunately I can get excited by a frock only when there is someone in it so I went to the middle floor, where there was a display of television sets. But since I've seen this sort of thing in Dixons, I carried on going to the ground floor, where there was a large queue to go in a triangular maze.

This is always going to be a problem with buildings of this nature, whether they be the Pompidou Centre in Paris or the Dome. What the hell can you put inside that is going to be more astonishing than the building itself?

The most successful exhibition ever staged in Bilbao was a motorcycle show. But then bikers tend not to be terribly interested in aesthetics. Most would walk over a lake of Renaissance art if there was a Harley-Davidson on the other side. I, on the other hand, was glad to be back outside again, to sit in a bar and gawp at this disjointed tower of titanium and golden limestone.

I knew that three architects had been invited to pitch for its design. Each was paid $10,000 and allowed three weeks and one site visit to come up with something. And I knew that the contract had been awarded to a Canadian called Frank Gehry. But who on earth paid for it?

The Guggenheims made a fortune from mining, but then they lost a big chunk of it when the South American mines they owned were nationalised.

Today the family is still a huge patron of the arts but it likes a bit of public money as well. And it got public money in Bilbao to the tune of $100 million.

And that begs another question. How can Bilbao, which is one of the greyest, most unfortunate and ugly towns in the whole world, possibly have come up with $100 million for a museum? Towns of this nature in Britain can't even afford to empty a dustbin let alone build a modern-day version of Westminster Abbey down by the river front.

This being Spain, answers are not easy to come by. Everyone has a recorded telephone message saying that they're at lunch and will be back some time in September. If by some miracle you do find someone who is at their desk, they say they can't be bothered to find out.

So let's consider the facts. Bilbao is a Basque town and the money was raised by the PNV, a Basque nationalist party. That's fine, but what is the PNV doing with access to $100 million?

I don't know – but I do know this: in 1999, and that's the most recent year for which figures are available, it cost the British taxpayer £3.5 billion to be a member of the European Union. That equates to £60 for every man, woman and child. And that sum, plus a bit more, went to Spain to help with the modernisation programme.

Well now, Spain already is modern. Dentists use

electricity. The hedges are neat and low-voltage lighting has replaced that halo of the Third World – the fluorescent tube. Sure, they may tell you that they've 'only' been a democracy for 25 years. But 25 years is a long time. Nobody ever says that he has 'only' been married for 25 years.

What are they doing with all the cash? Well, I can't find a link but it may well be that, actually, you and I paid for the Guggenheim. And that makes it as British as Gibraltar.

The Dome may have been an unmitigated disaster but it seems that, unwittingly, we've managed to create the greatest building the world has ever seen. Go there, but for two reasons don't go inside. One: it's not worth it; and two: they'll charge you, even though you've paid already.

Sunday 22 July 2001

They Speak the Language of Death in Basque Country

By the time you read this I'll be in Menorca, you'll be in Turkey, your neighbours will be in Florida and a man in a mask will be in your sitting room, helping himself to your television set.

Still, it could be worse. You could have gone to Biarritz. It was the world's first seaside resort and is to be found on the Atlantic coast just before western France makes a right-angled turn and becomes Spain. I love it there, and not just for the vast beach with those man-sized Atlantic rollers.

I love the town, which blends Napoleonic splendour with peeling Victorian modesty and I love the rolling hinterland, too, where you find the caves from which European man first stumbled 10,000 years ago. I love the cooking which tumbled into town from neighbouring Gascony. I love everything so much that I don't even mind the crummy weather that blights these parts from time to time.

Anyway, when it rains it's only a half-hour drive to Spain, where you can watch ballet dancers stab bulls. Then at night you can go to the town of San Sebastian, which has more bars per head of population than any other city in the world. Wellington's troops got so blotto, they burnt the whole place to the ground.

So what's wrong with it? Well, unfortunately, this is Basque country and that means it's twinned with a place that's up the Shining Path, along the Gaza Strip, past the Tamil's tiger, round Pol's Pot and beyond the Falls Road.

We tend to think of ETA, the Basque separatists, as a low-rent terrorist organisation which uses bicycle bombs because cars are too pricey. They're news in brief, at best.

Not when you're there, they're not. They raise money not by jangling tins in far-away Chicago but by making everyone, up to and including international footballers, pay a revolutionary tax. And if you don't pay, they blow up your car, your house, your wife, your budgerigar, your bar and everyone in it.

That's why I left the place behind and have come to Menorca.

Since the recent troubles began they have killed nearly 900 people and as a result there's a policeman on every street corner dressed up like Robocop, wielding a heavy machine-gun and sweating the sweat of a man who is very, very frightened indeed.

I saw one poor copper, a kid, probably eighteen years old, and I swear to God that if I had snuck up behind him and said 'Boo', he'd have had a heart attack. I'd only been there an hour before one of them was shot.

I'd only been there a day before I came round the corner to find myself at the scene of a car bomb. Now I've seen most things that can be done to a car, but it was quite a shock to see how far you can make one go, and in how many different directions, if you put a bit of dynamite under the driver's seat.

Needless to say, the driver in question had been turned into a veneer.

So that was two dead in a day and not even the Palestinians are at that level.

Yet ETA is still news in brief – unless British tourists are delayed flying home by the odd bomb, as in Malaga on Thursday.

How can this be? Spain is our next-door neighbour but one and yet, so far as I can tell, nobody in Britain has the first clue what these Basques actually want.

To try and find out, I spoke to Karmelo Landa, who is their equivalent of Gerry Adams and who quoted extensively from the book entitled *What To Say When You're the Spokesman for a Bunch of Terrorists*. It was all democratic this and political that and I must confess I got rather cross with him.

The fact is that the Basque region, apart from a short spell during the Spanish Civil War, has never been an autonomous state. They may be descended directly from those early cave dwellers but the Romans, the Vandals and the Visigoths passed them by. Since then, they claim to have discovered America, which is unlikely, and that they built the Armada, which sank. They also maintain that they gave the world the word 'silhouette'. But this isn't exactly up there with putting a man on the moon, is it?

The Basques have the same defining characteristics as the Welsh. The Welsh can sing. The Basques have big earlobes. The Welsh are good at moving stones. The Basques are all blood group O. And both have a militant core that wants autonomy primarily to protect a language that doesn't really work.

Welsh is burdened by an almost complete lack of vowels but it's nothing compared with the language of the Basque. Even the name of it is unpronounceable. Let me give you an example: the literal translation of 'I am writing' is 'In the act of writing, doing. You have me'. And to make matters worse, it seems that the only three letters in the Basque alphabet are X, K and X again. It's so hard that pretty well everyone, even in the Basque hill towns, prefers to use Spanish, despite the lisping and spitting.

It's madness. I can see why someone would fight for their freedom, god or country. But it's hard to see how a language can be worth a life. And nigh on impossible to see how Basque could be worth 900 lives.

Sunday 29 July 2001

Reason Takes a Bath in the Swimming Pool

The ninth week of my trip around Europe brings me to Menorca, where there is a harsh, laser edge to the shadows. The heat sits on everything out here with such oppressive force that even the crickets can't be bothered to sing. It should be relaxing.

Except it's not, because of course in the garden of the house I am borrowing there is a swimming pool which, after voicemail, is the single most exasperating rung on the ladder of human achievement.

It's funny, isn't it: nobody ever dreams of putting a pond in his garden. Ponds are for those who think it's safe to let their children play with electricity. Ponds are for pond life.

Barely a week goes by without a garden pond killing a toddler somewhere. But take away the lilies and the dragonflies, add a little depth for added danger, dye the whole thing vivid turquoise and suddenly we perceive the whole wretched thing to be as harmless as Lego.

The problem, however, with the pool out here in Menorca is not that it might kill the children. It's that it might kill me. There's a cover, you see, which adheres to the first rule of anything to do with swimming pools: it doesn't work. Not unless you dive underneath a wooden platform in the deep end and unjam the mechanism, a process that takes ten minutes – exactly nine minutes and fifty seconds longer than Mr Marlboro Man can hold his breath.

I've been down this road before. Five years ago I rented a house in the south of France which, it said in the blurb, came with a pool. And indeed it did. But on the second day of our holiday we awoke to find that half the water had escaped.

Keen to preserve what was left, I donned my Inspector Clouseau scuba suit and ascertained that the only possible way for water to leave the pool was via a big hole in the bottom. Unaware that this had something to do with filtration, I covered it with a large dinner plate and went to the beach.

Certainly, my brave and swift actions meant that no more water leaked away, but unfortunately they also meant that the pump was sucking on nothing for eight straight hours. People say the resultant explosion could be heard in Stuttgart.

I vowed there and then, and again this morning, that I would never have a pool at home, but unfortunately my wife really wants one.

'Why?' I wailed. 'You're Manx. You're supposed to have taste.'

'Yes,' she replied, 'but I was born in Surrey.'

There are other problems with installing a turquoise slash in our garden, chief among which is the fact that we live in Chipping Norton, widely regarded as the coldest town in England. Even when the whole country is basking under a ridge of pressure so high that everyone's eardrums are imploding, the only pool I ever want to immerse myself in is a nice hot bath.

But my wife is adamant and haughtily dismisses my suggestion of a skip filled with rainwater and slightly upended to create a deep end. I even suggested that we could heat it from below with a brazier, but she hit me over the head with a rolled-up newspaper. So I have been doing some research and it seems you can put in a chlorinated child-killer for £20,000 or so. That is less than I thought, but it's not enough.

There is a level of one-upmanship in pooldom that would leave a Cheshire car dealer breathless with envy. First of all there is the issue of temperature. Your pool must be warmer than anyone else's in The Close. But to win this game you end up with something that's hot enough to boil a lobster.

Then there's music. Moby must be piped into underwater speakers for reasons that I have yet to understand completely.

Let's not forget depth. A friend of mine called Jumbo recently installed a pool at his home on Hayling Island only to discover that it's impossible, when you're so close to the sea, to dig down more than 4 feet. He has ended up with a pool that has two shallow ends, connected in the middle with a shallow bit. You don't swim in it so much as stroll around looking like Jesus. It's social death.

The only way round it, I'm told, is to employ a pool man of such devastating beauty that nobody notices they are gathered round what is basically the most expensive puddle in Portsmouth.

But let's say that you have got a pool that is deeper than Lake Tahoe, hot enough to fry the underwater speakers, attended to by Hugh Grant and served by a pool house which is a full-scale model of the Taj Mahal. Then what?

Well, then you're going to need a pool cleaner. The best I ever saw was a huge spidery thing that waved its arms around, sucking up anything that drifted past. Its owner was very proud, and then very angry, when a friend of mine fed it a burger and it sank. 'What did you do that for?' he bellowed. 'Well,' said my friend, 'it serves you right for buying a cleaner that only eats leaves. How was I supposed to know it was vegetarian?'

So swimming pools can be summed up thus: they take all your money, all your sense of reason, all your time, and if you leave them alone for a moment they take your children as well.

Sunday 5 August 2001

You Can Fly an Awfully Long Way on Patience

I knew, of course, that a charter flight from some low-rent Spanish holiday resort to London's Stansted airport was never in a million years going to take off on time.

To make matters worse it had a scheduled departure of 11.30 p.m. which meant it would have had an entire day to get out of sync. And sure enough, when we arrived at the airport we were told it was still in Essex.

'So what's the problem this time?' I inquired with the world-weary resignedness of someone who has heard it all before. 'Technical problems? Wrong type of air? Leaves in the sky?' 'No,' said the rep, 'the captain got stuck in traffic on the M11.'

I see. Because the hopeless git did not set off for work on time, I now have to spend four hours in an overheated, understaffed departure lounge with seventy children under eight, none of whom is mine. Great.

I don't know who you are, captain, but I sincerely hope you have a penchant for Thai ladyboys and that your colleagues find out. I am not a vindictive man but it is my fervent wish that from now to the end of time all your itches are unreachable. And that someone writes something obscene in weedkiller on your front lawn.

To keep us all happy and to help to while away the

hours, we were assured that free soft drinks and snacks would be provided.

They were not. What was provided was a styrofoam cup of hot. Hot what, I'm not sure. It could have been tea or it could have been oxtail soup. The snack was a sandwich filled with a piece of pink that was thinner than the paintwork on a 1979 Lancia. Then I discovered that the batteries in my Game Boy were flat.

To my left, a fat family clad from head to foot in Adidas sportswear had managed to find some chips. An amazing achievement this, since all the shops were shut. But you could put people like that on the fourth moon of Jupiter and within fifteen minutes they would find a sack of King Edwards and a deep-fat fryer.

To my right there was a much thinner family, also clad in Adidas sportswear, attempting to get some sleep and using their Manchester United football shirts as pillows. Sleeping was difficult because every five minutes King Juan Carlos himself came on the Tannoy to explain very loudly that by royal decree smoking is prohibited.

Then it got more difficult still because a team of heroically lazy Spanish cleaners finally woke up from their afternoon siesta and decided that the floor needed a damn good polish, using a squadron of machines that were designed by the Russians in the 1950s and had been in service with the Angolan air force ever since.

By 1.30 a.m. I was reduced to reading the instructions on the fire extinguishers and contemplating starting a food fight. I decided against it because the bread in the free sandwiches was hard enough to kill and the filling was too light to fly properly. It would just sort of float.

At 1.45 a.m. we were asked by the king again to board buses which would take us to the plane. Yippee. At long last, Captain James T. Berk had arrived. We were on our way.

Oh no we weren't. After fifteen minutes of standing on the stationary bus, we were forced to endure 50 minutes of sitting on the stationary plane where there was no air conditioning and, worse still, no explanation or apology from the flight deck.

Only after we had become airborne and fallen asleep did Captain Fool come on the PA system to explain what had gone wrong. It had been too hot, he said, for the plane to take off and, as a result, some of the bags had been removed from the hold.

Oh, that's marvellous. So you get us home four hours late, you separate us from our luggage, you never say sorry and then you come up with the worst excuse I have ever heard. How can it have been too hot, you imbecile? Because of your shoddy timekeeping, it was three o'clock in the bloody morning.

The thing is, though, that I (mostly) kept my temper because I knew I could come home, write this and therefore make his life as miserable as he had made mine.

What staggered me was the patience of my fellow passengers. They never complained. They quietly sat at the airport eating their meat veneer. They quietly stood on the bus, sweating. They didn't even squeal when the stewardesses poured boiling water into their laps, told barefaced lies about the luggage being on board and generally treated us as if we were a nuisance in the smooth running of their aeroplane.

The problem is that we are used to all this, and more. We expect the tiny bit of road that isn't jammed solid to be festooned with speed cameras. We expect the train to be late and the Tube to explode. We know that the plane will make an unscheduled stop in Bogotá and that if we complain we'll be taken off by the police, arrested and shot.

Naturally, we expect a charter flight to get us back to Stansted four hours after everyone else because, of course, this particular airline is the sponsor of the spectacularly hopeless Minardi Formula One team which, last time I looked, was just finishing the 1983 French Grand Prix.

Sunday 12 August 2001

What I Missed on My Hols: Everyday Madness

And so, after two months on the Continent, I'm back in Britain trying to decide if I have missed anything. What I normally miss is the British weather. A dose of hot sunshine may be pleasant for a week or two, but soon you begin to tire of sunscreen and having a red nose. You find yourself hunting down bits of shade and not wanting to do any work because it's far too sweaty.

After four weeks I found myself lying awake at night dreaming of being cold. We have no idea how lucky we are in this country having weather that we don't notice; weather that doesn't slap us in the face every time we set foot outside the door.

But what concerns me more than the weather is what I've missed in the news. We all assume when we come back from a spell abroad that the country will have changed out of all recognition. There will have been fourteen days of developments about which we will have no knowledge.

New fashions will have come and gone. New political parties will have formed, new bands will have been created and we won't be able to talk about any of it at dinner parties. So what exactly have I missed in the past nine weeks?

I missed Bill Clinton standing in for Cliff Richard

at Wimbledon, and I missed the joyous spectacle of Jeffrey Archer going down, but then I didn't really because the verdict was extensively covered in the Spanish newspapers where, for some extraordinary reason, he was likened to a modern-day Oscar Wilde. Well yes, apart from being conspicuously un-gay and even more conspicuously unable to write.

Also, I missed Madonna's deification. When I left she was a fading Detroit pop star but I've come back to find that she is sharing a social plinth with a fat blonde hairdresser from Wales who seems to have become famous after admitting to a fondness for blinking. The foreign newspapers missed that one. Perhaps they were diverted with the problems in the Middle East.

It seems that I also missed a hugely funny television programme about child pornography, although I'm told that most of the people who found it offensive missed it too.

Then there has been this business with Michael Portillo. When I left he was going to be leader of the Conservative Party. But now the clever money seems to be on some bloke who I've never heard of. Is he good at blinking as well? One has to hope not or he might miss himself.

I was about to deduce that I had missed nothing when my eye was caught by the New Labour exhibition at the Saatchi Gallery in London. What on earth were they exhibiting? Perhaps they had taken a leaf out of Tracey Emin's book. Perhaps this is where all the National Health Service beds went. And all the bricks that should have been used to build playcentres for the kiddies. As well as the last vestiges of our pride and dignity.

Have you ever heard of anything quite so preposterous as an exhibition, in a world-renowned art gallery, that is named after the ruling political party? A party that received fewer votes than the girl who likes blinking.

But, that said, I would love more than anything to do my own New Labour exhibition. 'This is the egg that hit Mr Prescott and here's the shirt worn by Tony when he had the sweat problem. And if you follow me now past the Women's Institute zone, we can see Peter Mandelson's mortgage-application form, lovingly entwined with Reinaldo's visa-waiver document.'

In the restaurant I would have lots of mugs, lots of mad cows and lots of free fish for the Spanish visitors. In the play zone I would have hundreds of savage, rabid foxes and a helter-skelter. If anyone said that wasn't very New Labour, I would tell them it was a spiral staircase for disabled people. Inside I would have Ron Davies in the lavatories, Keith Vaz on the till and audio guides recorded by Michael Martin. And when it all went horribly wrong I would blame Mo Mowlam.

Keen to find out what had actually been exhibited at the gallery and if I was on the right track, I dug out an old copy of *Time Out* and was somewhat bewildered to find it had singled out a video exhibit by Liane Lang. Who she is, I have no idea. Another *Big Brother* contestant perhaps?

My bewilderment turned to bafflement when I read what the video contains: a clay hand manipulates a woman's groin fringed with spiky black hair. Devoid of sexiness, the image, we are assured, is perplexing. You're damn right it's perplexing. And it gets worse. Rebecca Warren, it says here, uses clay to a more playful and seductive effect. Painted with a wash of pink, a woman opens her legs to the lascivious attentions of what might be a grey dog.

Astonished, I telephoned the gallery and asked what any of this had to do with Tony Blair and his third way. 'Oh, nothing,' said the girl. 'It's just that the exhibition opened on election day and we sort of thought the New Labour name fitted.' Actually, it does.

It's a load of metropolitan claptrap. I may have missed the exhibition, which closes today, but to be honest I didn't miss it at all.

Sunday 19 August 2001

Rule the Waves? These Days We're Lost at Sea

My childhood memories of Britain's maritime achievements centre around endless black-and-white television pictures of shrivelled up little men with faces like Furball XL5 stumbling off their battered yachts in Southampton having sailed round the world backwards.

Francis Chichester, Chay Blyth, Robin Knox Johnston. Grainy pictures of Cape Horn. And Raymond Baxter reminding us all that, once again, the noble island nation has tamed the savage ferocity of those southern oceans. Trafalgar, Jutland. The Armada etc. etc. etc. Britannia rules the waves. Always has, always will. The end.

Now, however, we find that pretty well every sailing record in the book is held by the French. They've been across the Atlantic faster than anyone else, round the world faster than anyone else and, while plucky Ellen MacArthur grabbed all the headlines by pluckily coming second in the recent Vendée Globe race, the event was actually won by a Frog. Same as it was the year before. And the year before that.

Some say the problem is sponsorship, some argue that sailing in Britain is drowning in its own gin and tonic. But the simple fact is that, these days, the only time a British sailor gets on the news is when his boat sinks.

We had that bloke who turned turtle off Australia and survived by eating himself. Then there's the Royal Navy which, these days, would struggle to gain control of a puddle. And let's not forget Pete Goss, whose Team Phillips boat, built to go round the world, didn't even get round Land's End before the end came off.

Now I should make it perfectly clear at this point that I'm not a sailor. I tried it just the once on what was basically an aquatic Rover 90. It was captained by an enthusiastic Hampshire type who kept saying we were really 'knocking on', but I doubted this, since I was being overtaken by my cigarette smoke.

You could have steered that bloody thing through a hurricane and it would still have only done four knots. And that's another thing. Why do people lose the ability to speak English as soon as they cast off the spring? Why is speed knots and knots reefers? And why, every time you settle back for a real reefer, do you have to get up again? To get the painters in.

Furthermore, even the most mild-mannered man acts like he's got the painters in as soon as he grabs the wheel (helm). Why? We're at sea, for heaven's sake. If I don't respond immediately to your commands or pull a sheet instead of a halyard, it really won't matter. A two-second delay will not cause us to crash.

In fact, come to think of it, I know all there is to know about sailing, i.e. that it means spending the day at 45 degrees while moving around very slowly and being shouted at.

Understandably, then, I was a trifle reluctant when I was invited to Brest, to join the captain and crew of *Cap Gemini*, a £3-million French-built monster – the biggest, fastest trimaran the world has ever seen.

Launched just last month, it is hoped it will get round the world in 60 days and, to put that in perspective, an American nuclear submarine just made the same trip in 83 days. This is one really fast boat.

But it's the sheer size of the thing which draws the crowds. Finding it in a port is a bit like finding a haystack in a needle. You just look for the mast which stretches up past the other masts, through the troposphere and way into the magnetosphere. This boat doesn't need satellite navigation. You just climb up that mast and have a look.

In fact, *Cap Gemini* doesn't really have anything. To keep the weight down, the whole boat, even the sail, is made from carbon fibre and so, having gone to all that trouble and expense, they weren't going to undo it with internal luxuries. The ten meat machines who sail it are expected to use their clothes for mattresses. And it doesn't even have a lavatory.

We set off and, for five glorious minutes, I think I saw the appeal of this sailing business. The sun came out, the wind picked up and the mighty yacht set off into the Bay of Biscay like a scalded cock. Perched on one of the three hulls, 20 feet clear of the iron-flat sea, I could scarcely believe my eyes as the speedometer climbed past 30, 35 and then 40 knots. Using nothing but the wind for power, we were doing nearly 50 miles per hour. This was astonishing. Had I been an American, I would have made whooping noises.

But then the wind died down again and we turned for home. Except of course we didn't. This being a sailing boat we had to endlessly tack back up the estuary, turning what should have been a 25-kilometre breeze into a 3-hour, 50-kilometre, aimless, walking-pace slog.

There was nothing to eat, nothing to drink, nothing to smoke and, no matter where I went, some fantastically good-looking hunk of sun-bleached muscle trod on me and then shouted because I was in its way. This, I think, is why the British have largely given up with sailing.

Apart from a few crashing bores in blazers, the rest of us have realised that, for getting round the world these days, you can't beat an Airbus. Which is also French. Dammit.

Sunday 2 September 2001

Why Can't We Do Big or Beautiful Any More?

With the England football team on the crest of a wave and unemployment at an all-time low, it should be a good time to sit back, put on some Elgar and feel warmly fuzzy about being British.

Concorde is coming back, too, and soon it will be tearing across the Atlantic twice a day to remind Johnny Yank that, once upon a time, we were capable of unbelievable genius. Even NASA's most respected engineers have admitted to me, in private, that designing and building a supersonic airliner was a greater technological challenge than putting a man on the moon.

So it's wonderful that once again Heathrow will rumble and shudder under the onslaught of those massive Olympus jets. However, it's also a little sad because you can bet your last cornflake that the British won't have anything to do with man's next great landmark.

The problem is that the twenty Concordes cost £1.5 billion, which back then was an astronomical fortune. Even today it would buy two Millennium Domes. Yet despite this, the last five to roll off the production lines were sold for just FFr1 each.

The whole project was driven by Tony Benn, a man who was also responsible for getting the hovercraft out of Cockerell's shed and into the Channel. In addition, he helped to create ICL, Britain's answer to America's IBM. When he was postmaster-general, he pushed for the Post Office Tower which, for twenty or more years, was London's tallest building.

Denis Healey once said that Benn 'came close to destroying the Labour Party as a force in twentieth-century British politics'. And I bet he had few friends at the Treasury either. But my God, he knew how to make everyone feel good about being British.

Today, however, the government doesn't give. It simply counts the cost. Everything is measured in terms of how many baby incubators it could have bought or how many teachers it might have paid for.

You just know that if Norwich city council were to build a beautiful fountain in the city centre, the local newspaper would find some bereaved mother to come out from behind the Kleenex to say the money should have been spent on speed humps instead.

Part of the problem with the Dome was that instead of making a monument that would stand for all of time, they tried to make it a short-term business proposition whose basic function was to pay for itself. And while the London Eye has been a resounding success, you know that its foundations are rooted in someone's profit and loss account.

Maybe this is a fundamental problem with capitalism. Maybe the people of a country don't get blanketed in the warm glow of national pride unless they have a socialist at the helm. Someone like Benn. Or the man who dreamt up those Soviet May Day parades.

Certainly the communist cities I've visited do give good monument.

However, to disprove this theory there is the Grande Arche de la Défense in the not very communist city of Paris. Had they filled the middle with offices, the rental income would have been boosted tenfold, but then they wouldn't have ended up with something so utterly magnificent. And what about the very non-communist US Navy? There is no practical reason on earth why it needs fourteen city-sized aircraft carriers. They exist primarily to instil in the folks back home a sense of security and national pride.

So I'm left facing the inescapable conclusion that the lack of will to build something worthwhile, something beautiful, something brilliant, is a uniquely British problem. Maybe we can't feel a sense of pride in ourselves because we don't know who or what we are any more.

The prime minister is a Labour Tory. There's a mosque at the end of your street and a French restaurant next door. We are neither in nor out of Europe. We are famous for our beer but we drink in wine bars. We are not a colonial power but we still have a commonwealth. We are jealous of the rich but we buy into the *Hello!* celebrity culture. We live in a United Kingdom that's no longer united. We are muddled.

And this must surely be the only country in the world that sees its national flag as a symbol of oppression. So if you can't be seen as patriotic for fear of being labelled a racist, you aren't going to be desperately inclined to build something for the good of the nation. Not that you know what the nation actually is or means any more.

Our football team may be on its way to the World Cup finals but we don't even have a national stadium in which it can play home games.

Concorde is back in the air – but not because the great white bird makes us all feel good. It's back because the accountants at British Airways have turned the white elephant into a dirty great cash cow.

To combat this disease, I would like to see a fund set up that does nothing but pay for great public buildings, follies, laser shows, towers, fountains, airships, aqueducts. Big, expensive stuff designed solely to make us go 'wow'. I even have a name for this fund. We could call it the lottery.

Sunday 9 September 2001

Learn from Your Kids and Chill Out Ibiza-Style

You may have seen various Ibiza-style compilation music albums advertised in the middle of fairly highbrow television programmes recently. And you may have thought that this was as inappropriate as advertising knickers in the middle of a football match. You are watching a documentary about insects. You are intelligent. The only Ibiza soundtrack that you're interested in is the cicadas, not the mega-decibel noise coming out of the clubs.

I mean, take an album called *The Chillout Session* which, according to the blurb on the cover, is a laid-back mix of blissful beats and chilled-out house featuring Jakatta, Leftfield, William Orbit, Groove Armada, Underworld and Bent. Dotcom computerised e-music for the e-generation. Or, to put it another way, rubbish.

And rightly so. It has always been the job of modern music to annoy parents. When I used to watch *Top of the Pops* in the early 1970s my father's face would adopt the look of a man who'd just been stabbed in the back of the neck with a screwdriver. There was bewilderment and some real pain, too, especially during 'Ballroom Blitz'.

This was a man who spoke the language of pop music with the élan with which I speak French. He used the definite article indiscriminately, talking about the Queen and the T Rex. He referred to the Rod Stewart as 'that man who sings while he's on the lavatory', and once said of the Billy Idol: 'You'd have thought if he was going on television, he'd have put a shirt on.'

He honestly and truthfully could not see any difference at all between Rick Wakeman and Rick Derringer. I could never believe it, but to his ears, Mick Fleetwood and Mick Jagger were one and the same.

And yet twenty years down the line, I found myself in the same boat, unable to tell the difference between the house and the garage. Techno, hip-hop, rap. It was all the same to me. A collection of angry-looking young men with their trousers on back to front, urging us to go out and kill a pig.

This is undoubtedly why Radio 2 became the world's most listened-to station. Thanks to an appealing blend of Terry Wogan and the Doobie Brothers, it was a little haven of peace for the fortysomething music lover who was terrified of the noises being made on Radio 1.

However, if you listen exclusively to Radio 2, you are isolated from the fast-moving world of modern music. You become stuck in a Neil Young Groundhog Day, endlessly buying *After the Gold Rush* on CD and mini disc.

You don't watch MTV. You don't read the *NME*. You don't see *Top of the Pops* any more. So, how do you know when there's some new music out there that you would like?

The record companies can't put flyers under the windscreen wipers of every Volvo in the land, so that's why these *Ibiza Chillout* records are being advertised in the middle of programmes you like to watch. It's because they feature the type of music you would like to hear.

You may not have heard of William Orbit but you will know his song well because it's Barber's *Adagio for Strings*. And while you may be unfamiliar with Groove Armada, you'll be able to hum along because you've heard their tune on and on in those slow-motion end-of-championship slots on *Grandstand*.

Listening to this music is like having a length of ermine pulled through your head. If honey could make a noise, this is what it would sound like. It becomes the perfect soundtrack for your spag bol and Chianti supper party.

Of course, you're not going to listen to it in the same way that you listened to Steve Miller's *Fly Like an Eagle* in 1976. Back then, listening to an album was a job in itself whereas this e-music is acoustic wallpaper, something you have on while you do something else. In our language, it's Jean-Michel Jarre meets Mike Oldfield, without the joss sticks and the vinyl crackle.

Moby is particularly good. Buy *I Like to Score* tomorrow morning and you'll never listen to Supertramp again. You'll retune your car stereo to Radio 1 and you'll put up with five hours of pig killing for five minutes of the whale song.

And you'll start to hear other bands that you like. Radiohead. Toploader. Coldplay. Dido. David Gray. Stereophonics. You may have heard the names over the past few years and you may have assumed, as I did, that they banged garden furniture into computers and recorded road drills for the benefit of your children, but no. You'll hear melodies that will cause you to hum along. And none of them will encourage you to stab a policeman.

I've taken to buying their albums and it's wonderful not having to stand at the counter in a record shop being called 'man' by the spiky salesman because I want *The Yes Album* on CD.

But if middle-aged people are able to discuss the latest mega-mix from Ibiza and the vocal range of Joe Washbourne from Toploader then our children will have nowhere to go. We'll be in Ibiza giving it large and, to rebel, they'll be on a Hoseasons canal boat singing songs from *The Sound of Music*.

Sunday 16 September 2001

Going to the Dentist in the Teeth of All Reason

Left to its own devices, an elephant would never die. It has no natural enemies. It is not prone to riding a motorcycle. It has the metabolic rate of granite. So, to ensure that the world was not eventually overrun by herds of immortal two-tonners, nature put a time bomb in its mouth: weak teeth. They are replaced with new ones every ten years, but when the sixth set has worn out, that's it. Game over for Nellie.

Human beings are different. The enamel that coats our teeth is not only the hardest substance in our bodies but also one of the toughest and most resilient concoctions found anywhere on planet Earth.

Think about it. The oldest evidence of humanoid existence was found three years ago just outside Johannesburg. Named Little Foot, nothing much remains. It's just a sort of fossil, except for the teeth which loom out of the rock as fresh and as shiny as they were when the poor creature lived, 3.6 million years ago.

We see this all the time. Archaeologists are forever pulling dead priests out of fields in Lincolnshire and declaring that they died during the Reformation after being boiled in acid, burnt, hung, drawn, quartered, crushed and then quartered again for good measure.

Every bone is always smashed and rotten and yet the teeth still gleam.

So why, then, has the government recently announced that it will be allocating £35 million to help eradicate tooth decay? Why did it say that poor children can now get free toothbrushes on the National Health Service? Well, it's because the health minister who dreamt up these schemes is called Hazel Blears. This would make her a woman. And that would make her completely obsessed with other people's teeth.

When I was a single man I went to the dentist only once, when I had toothache. He said all my teeth would have to be filled except two, which would need root canals. Then, after he had filled my face with needles and Novocaine, he asked whether I would like the work done privately or on the NHS.

'Oor's huh diffence?' I tried to say.

'Well,' he replied with a sneer, 'if you have it done privately, the fillings will match your teeth. And if you have it done on Mrs Thatcher, they won't.'

I had seen Mrs T's teeth so, poor as I was, I went private.

For the next fifteen years I didn't go to the dentist at all and it made not the slightest bit of difference. I was not visited by the Itosis family and their troublesome son, Hal. On the rare occasions when I managed to get girls back to my flat, they did not keel over and die when I moved in for the first kiss. Some didn't faint.

Then along came my wife, who spends 60 per cent of the family's GDP on electric toothbrushes and 40 per cent of her morning sawing away with floss. Also, she sends me off for a dental check-up every six months.

Why do I need to have a man poke about in my mouth with a sharpened screwdriver when I know that my teeth will last about 50,000 years longer than the rest of me?

Nobody dies of tooth decay. It's always some other part of the body that gives up, but despite this we don't go to the doctor twice a year demanding a full service. Come on, doc, there's nothing obviously wrong but I want you to examine every single bit of me minutely. I want X-rays and then I want to see your hygienist, who will spray jets of ice-cold grit up my backside.

No, we go to the doctor only when something is wrong and that's how it should be at the dentist.

Vanity is the problem. Nobody will be able to see if your spleen has a growth on it the size of a cabbage, but when your molars go brown and gingivitis takes your gums, that's a woman's idea of hell on earth.

There are four different types of teeth. There are canines which are used for tearing off lumps of meat. There are incisors which are used for cutting it. There are premolars for crushing it. And there are American teeth which are used for appearing in *Hello!* magazine.

You do not achieve American teeth with toothpaste and regular flossing. Nor will you have the full Victoria Beckham after a course of bleaching at the dentist. No, to achieve teeth which are way better than anything nature ever intended, what you need is millions of pounds.

Small wonder that in a football wall these days, the vain and effeminate players put their hands over their mouths rather than their testicles.

There are other drawbacks, too. I'm told that you will emerge from the operation not only looking different but sounding like a different person as well. And there's no way of knowing before the dentist starts work with his chisel whether you'll emerge from the ordeal as Stephen Hawking or Sue Ellen.

All we do know is that people with American gnashers all look exactly the same. If you are horribly injured in an accident, they won't be able to identify you from your teeth because they will have come from the same box in Beverly Hills as everyone else's. Think about the consequences: you may spend the rest of time lying beneath a gravestone which tells passers-by that you were Victoria Beckham.

Sunday 23 September 2001

Sea Duel with the Fastest Migrants in the West

I've often thought as I've watched the police prise yet another frightened little brown man with a moustache from the underside of a Eurostar train: 'How bad must life have been at home for that to have been better?'

According to the union that represents the immigration service, the ISU, there are now 1.2 million illegal immigrants living in Britain, and we know full well, of course, how they got here. They were ushered into the tunnel and into the backs of trucks by the French police.

However, what I've always wanted to know is: how the hell are they getting into Europe in the first place? Where's the leak?

Well, last week, I found it. Every month, thousands of immigrants are being brought by the Albanian mafia in fast boats across the 50-mile-wide Strait of Otranto from Albania into southern Italy.

And what are the Italian police doing to stop them? Well, I had a good look round and, so far as I can tell, the most important thing they have done so far is buy themselves some really cool sunglasses. It's like a Cutler and Gross convention.

And you should see their patrol boats. Forget super-yacht alley in Antibes. Forget the Class One racers. The fastest, sleekest machines I've ever seen are backed up to the harbour wall in Otranto, rocking as the mighty diesels are revved.

So, the police look good and they can go really fast. But unfortunately they can't go fast enough.

You see, the profits from smuggling people are simply mind-boggling. The going rate for the one-way trip is $800 (£540) per person, and with 40 people to a boat, that works out at $32,000 (about £21,600) a go. And a few $32,000 trips buys you an awful lot of horsepower.

To combat this, the police are now allowed to keep the boats they catch and use them against the smugglers. Which means the mafia have to build, or steal, faster boats to stay ahead.

Welcome, then, to the biggest aquatic race track the world has ever seen. A race track where the victors win the chance to spend the rest of their days above a chip shop in Bradford, and the losers end up dead.

Here's the problem. As soon as a mafia boat sets off from Albania it is picked up by Italian radar stations, which direct police boats towards the target. But even if they can go fast enough to catch up, then what?

You can't simply ask the driver to pull over, because he won't. He's going hell for leather and won't stop even when he reaches the beach. You might be able to block him but then – and this happens a lot – he'll lob the cargo of Kurds over the side, and once they've drowned turn and run for the lawlessness of home.

There's only one solution and that's to point your 80-mph boat at the mafia's 90-mph boat, and do what your forefathers did when they were Romans. Ram it.

This is spectacularly dangerous. Last year, fourteen immigrants were killed when they were hit by a police boat, and earlier this year, when the mafia used similar tactics to evade capture, three policemen died.

And really, is the risk worth it? I mean, the poor passengers on these boats sold everything they had for their one shot at freedom, so what chance do they have when they're sent back after 30 days in a holding station? They'll be penniless and homeless in a country where, according to the Italian police, there simply is no sense of right and wrong. Just rich and poor.

And besides, the mafia is now running a marketing campaign pinched, I think, from Ryanair. If you get caught on your first trip, they give you two more rides. But there are strings attached – well, chains, actually. If you make it, you'll owe them a debt; a debt that will never be repaid by hanging around on Regent Street washing windscreens.

You're going to have to get into some serious stealing and robbing to keep your benefactors happy.

They're going to put your sister on the streets and your daughters are going to be burnt with cigarettes, whipped and put on the internet.

So what's to be done? We can't let them all in, but by the same token it goes beyond the bounds of human decency to keep them all out.

David Blunkett spoke last week about relaxing the laws on immigrants, allowing people with a special skill to get a work permit in Britain. Great, but the people coming over on those boats are not teachers and computer programmers. All they can do is strip down an AK47 and milk a goat.

The danger is all they're going to learn while they're over here is how to remove a Panasonic stereo from the dashboard of a Ford Orion.

To stop this happening, we must go after the people who put these poor souls in debt even before they get here. We must go after the mafia. Of course, 4,500 British troops have been in Macedonia for months, trying to do just that. But last week, as Tony Blair spoke about his dream of waging an international war against terror and injustice, the soldiers packed their bags and came home.

And now the mafia will be rubbing its hands with glee, knowing that pretty soon half of Afghanistan is going to roll up at the Albanian seaside . . .

Sunday 7 October 2001

My Verdict? Juries are As Guilty As Hell . . .

This week various civil-liberty types have been running around as though they're on fire because new government proposals would strip a defendant of his or her automatic right to trial by jury. The plans say that if you're charged with a medium-level offence such as theft or assault or doing 41 mph, then you would be tried by a judge and two magistrates.

What's wrong with that? Whenever I meet someone new I take in the little details, the hair, the shoes, the eyes, and within five seconds have decided whether I like them or not. In normal everyday life it doesn't matter that nine times out of ten I'm wrong. But it would matter a very great deal if I were to make one of these lightning decisions while serving on a jury.

The defence team could argue until they were blue in the face that their client was in Morocco on the day of the crime. They could show me tickets proving that he was and wheel out David Attenborough and Michael Palin as character witnesses. But I'm sorry, if I didn't like the look of the defendant's trousers then he'd better get used to the idea of communal showers for a while.

I know people, people with bright eyes and clean hair, who have done exactly the same sort of thing while on jury service. They've told me afterwards that they didn't listen to a word that was said because it was obvious, from the moment the defendant walked in, that he was as guilty as sin: 'You could tell just by looking at him. He had a beard and everything.'

Furthermore, I know people who shouldn't be allowed anywhere near a courtroom because, quite frankly, the inkwells would be more capable of making a rational decision.

I heard a woman on a radio quiz the other day say the two counties that border Devon are 'Yorkshire and the Falkland Islands'. And the country is full of people who regularly, and quite deliberately, watch soap operas. I once met a girl who thought there were two moons and that mosquitoes could burrow through walls. As the law stands, she could have been selected to try Ernest Saunders.

John Wadham, director of Liberty, the civil-liberties group, said the abolition of juries amounted to an attack on fairness in the criminal justice system. But what, pray, is fair about being tried by someone who thinks that insects can operate Black & Decker two-speed hammer drills?

And what's fair about asking me to sit on one of those fraud trials that go on for twelve months? Well, it won't happen. If I'm asked, I shall simply misbehave in front of the judge on the first day because, believe me, doing a month in clink for contempt beats the hell out of sitting on a school bench for a year listening to men in wigs arguing about tax in a language I don't understand.

Unless a fraud case is clear-cut, by which I mean the

white male defendant tried to cash a cheque in the name of Mrs Nbongo, then no normal person on earth could possibly be expected to reach a fair and reasonable decision.

Think about it. A Cambridge-educated genius spends fifteen years perpetrating a stunning piece of tax avoidance. Then some of the best legal brains in the country conclude that it was, in fact, evasion. And who decides which side is right? A bunch of people from McDonald's and Kwik-Fit. You may as well roll the dice.

Surely, therefore, it must be a good idea to let judges decide for themselves whether a jury, even in the crown court, would necessarily be a good thing.

For sure there are some judges who can't get through the day without dropping a clanger. Just this week, someone who had been sent to jail by magistrates for three months was released by a judge who said, and I'm quoting now: 'Prison doesn't do anyone any good.' But even a buffoon as idiotic as this would know how many moons there are.

Let's be honest. To qualify as a judge you must have displayed, at some point in your life, an above-average level of staying power. Whereas I couldn't get even halfway through my libel lectures at journalism college before I was filled with an uncontrollable urge to fall asleep.

All things considered, I think the use of judges and magistrates will make these new district courts fairer, faster and cheaper. But there are some aspects to the proposals that must have been dreamt up by one of the more stupid audiences on *Who Wants to be a Millionaire?*

I can't see the point of mix 'n' matching the tone of the judge's skin to that of the defendant, and I really can't understand the new ideas on so-called plea bargaining. The proposal is that the sooner you plead guilty the more lenient your sentence will be. Come running out of the jeweller's shouting 'It was me, it was me' and they'll let you off with a light birching. But plead not guilty to a judge who thinks you are and you'll be showering with other men for the rest of time.

Still, all this is likely to become law, so on that basis I'd like to say that I'm going to London tomorrow morning and will be driving on the M40, between junctions eight and one, at speeds in excess of 95 mph.

Sunday 14 October 2001

The More We're Told the Less We Know

Every day we are bombarded with surveys that tell us what the nation is thinking. These help shape government and corporate policy. Yet the people who are being questioned – you and me – have no clue what we're talking about.

We drown these days under the weight of information coming into our homes. We have the internet and rolling television news. We in Britain read more papers than any other European country. But the more we're told, the less we know.

Think about it. When you are twenty you know everything. But the more you travel, and the more you learn and the more you read, the more you realise that, actually, the more you know, the more you know nothing.

Take the war in Kosovo. As far as I could tell, it was an absurd venture. A whole bunch of tribes had been knocking eight bells out of one another since time began, when all of a sudden, NATO decided, for no obvious reason, that the Serbs needed a damn good bombing.

Confident that I'd got it all worked out, I voiced this opinion to an American called James Rubin. He'd actually worked with Madeleine Albright in the Balkans and very probably had Slobodan's number programmed into his mobile. But what the hell, I'd had a few wines and I was ready for a scrap.

And what a scrap it turned out to be. He may have had all the information but I'd had all the Chablis. So he destroyed me. He peeled my argument like an orange. In boxing terms, it was like Lennox Lewis going head to head with Charlotte Church.

Now we spool forward a few weeks to another dinner party where I used Rubin's argument on the man to my left. Unfortunately, he was an American banker who, it turned out, had brokered some sort of deal between the telephone system in Serbia and the Pope. Once again I found myself in the Charlotte Church role, reeling from the twin hammer blows of reason and knowledge.

So, if you walk up to me in the street now and ask whether I think the current campaign in Afghanistan is a good or a bad thing, I shall have to say that I don't know.

My gut feeling is that America should divert its considerable resources to setting up a Palestinian state, but since these views coincide almost exactly with those that are expressed in the *Guardian* every day, it's almost certain I'm wrong.

How will I ever know, when all we get are soundbites and speculation and surveys that tell us that 107 per cent of the world think Tony Blair is God? And 0 per cent think he's a buffoon on a massive and dangerous ego trip. But then did you know that 72 per cent of all statistics are made up on the spur of the moment? Including that one.

So, on that basis, what do we think about the euro? The surveys suggest that 80 per cent or so are against, with about 18 per cent in favour. Which means that only 2 per cent of the population are clever enough to realise they simply don't know.

Last year I thought it was as stupid as trying to build the roof of the house before you'd built the walls. Then I spent the entire summer travelling around Europe from the Polish border with Germany to the northwestern tip of Spain; from Brest in Brittany to the tip of Italy. And I decided that we have a lot more to learn from our European neighbours than they do from us. Good coffee, for instance. And better pornography in hotel bedrooms.

'So,' said a girl I had dinner with last weekend, 'you'd let Poland in?' 'Yes,' I said. 'You'd let all the eastern European states in?' 'Yes.' 'Including Albania?' 'Well, all of them except Albania,' I said. 'And Macedonia?' 'And Macedonia,' I conceded, realising that after six months on a fact-finding tour of the Continent, absorbing knowledge like a sponge, I'd come home with a half-formed thought.

It turns out, however, that before a state can join the union, it must comply with a set of rules and terms so complicated that they run to seventeen volumes. And now I know that what I know is that I know nothing at all.

Someone out there knows, but he's only ever given three seconds on the evening news to explain. So he comes up with a soundbite that nourishes our quest for knowledge with the effectiveness of a McNugget.

I have a similar problem with the environment. I read more scientific studies than most and I've always thought it's just a bunch of anticapitalist nonsense to suggest that we're all going to suffocate by next Wednesday. But last week I sat in that thick brown smog that has turned the south of France from the Côte d'Azur into the Côte de Brun and thought: hang on a minute. This has not been created by all the sailing boats.

By doing some research and giving it some thought, I'd turned a firmly held conviction into one side of an intercranial debate.

The inescapable conclusion to all this is that if you have all the facts to hand, you will see there are two sides to every argument and that both sides are right. So, you can only have an opinion if you do not have all the facts to hand. This certainly explains the *Guardian*.

Sunday 21 October 2001

Without a PR Protector, I'm Just Another Fat Git

Well, I'm back from holiday pink and perky, thank you very much. But then, of course, you knew that, because while I was away the *Sunday Mirror* ran a picture of me on the beach in Barbados.

The accompanying story suggested that I was celebrating my new £1-million contract with the BBC, that I was staying at the world-famous Sandy Lane hotel which costs £8,000 a night, and that I have become fat. 'Pot Gear' said the rather clever headline.

It was all jolly interesting except my contract is not worth £1 million, I was not staying at the Sandy Lane and it doesn't cost £8,000 a night. Furthermore, they completely missed the big story. One of the biggest stories ever, in fact. The reason why I'm so fat is because I'm pregnant.

Well, that's what happens when you get shafted isn't it? The problem here, of course, is that the photographer never actually came along and asked why I was there, in which case I would have told him the joyful news about my amazing new baby. He just hid in a bush with a long tom lens.

Do I mind? No, not really. It's quite flattering to think my stomach is more important than a dead Queen Mother and a war in the Middle East. But what interests

me is that the next day another newspaper ran some
pictures of Gary Lineker on a beach in Barbados. Fine,
except that instead of describing him as a jug-eared
midget, they said he was a lovely, adorable, happy-clappy
family man.

Why? We both have the same employer. We were
both with our children, on the same island, at the same
time. Neither of us is known to the people who wrote
the stories. So why am I a rich, fat git squandering
licence-fee payers' money at the world's worst hotel,
while Lineker is a churchwarden whose tireless work for
charity has resulted in thousands of orphaned children
being brought back from the dead, and ended several
small wars.

Well, I've made some calls and it seems that Gary
employs a public relations person – a former editor of
the *Sun* no less – to create and mould and manage press
coverage. While I don't.

And this, I think, is the root cause of all the recent
aggravation with Naomi Campbell and the *Mirror*, the
stories about Les Dennis and Amanda Holden, and whoever it was went off with the captain of Blackburn Rovers.
No wait. One of them was a drug addict, weren't they? I
can't remember.

The point is that pretty well all celebs live behind a
PR net curtain and enjoy the diffused light it creates.
They're used to the *OK!*-type feature where they're
seen at home, cutting up a freshly baked nut loaf with
some shiny apples on the coffee table. They only need
roll a 2p piece into a lifeboat-charity box at a pub and

they're painted in the papers the next day as a sort of Paul Getty, but better looking and with nicer breasts.

So when a paper catches them with a line of coke up their schnozzers or a dead builder in the swimming pool, it's like they've been thrust through the curtain and are facing the real world for the first time. It's nasty.

PR is nasty, too, but unfortunately it works. Not only for celebrities but also for politicians. It alone put a completely unprincipled man in No. 10, and even more amazingly it kept him there.

All those useless meddlers on the front bench have been on PR courses to make them more eloquent and better able to deal with the press. Well, all except one, of course, and as a result he's projected as a fat, pugilistic twerp with two Jags.

Big business uses it, too. Twice now I've attacked the Vauxhall Vectra and twice the enormous General Motors PR division has managed to spin the story round so that I emerged as the villain of the piece. Again. And he's fat, you know.

The thing is though that PR is not desperately expensive. Press inquiries can be handled for maybe £500 a month, whereas for £2,000 you can expect to be given your own personal halo and some wings. So why, I wonder, do we not use it in everyday life?

Night after night, my children go to bed angry with me for one reason or another. Usually because I've made them go to bed. So why don't I get a PR girl to do it for me: 'Your daddy wants you to stay up all night and eat chocolate, but Mummy says it's bedtime.'

Then when I inadvertently put all the crockery in the tumble dryer – it happens – my PR person could bury the bad news on a day when one of the kids has fallen off a swing and cut her knee.

Late for a meeting? Ordered 2 million paperclips by mistake? Goosed the boss's wife at a Christmas party? All of these things can be spun to your advantage if you get yourself your own personal Alastair Campbell.

I'm certainly going to get a PR man when my new baby is born. Because if I try to handle things myself, I'll end up making a mess of it. I can imagine the story in *Hello!* now: 'Jeremy Clarkson invites us to his dirty house for the birth of his fourth hideous child.'

Sunday 14 April 2002

Why Have an Argument? Let's Say It with Fists

This summer the Albert Hall in London will play host to an evening of 'ultimate fighting'. Described as an extreme test for mind and body, the participants are billed as modern-day Roman gladiators; except of course nobody gets eaten.

Ultimate fighting is an American import, naturally, and the idea is that two men are locked in a metal cage where they knock eight bells out of each other using whatever discipline happens to be handiest at the time – kick boxing, kung fu, wrestling, punching, judo. The only things which are not allowed are eye-gouging, and anything involving the groin or the throat. It does not say anything about teeth, though, so who knows – maybe someone will get eaten.

Predictably, every wishy-washy liberal is up in arms, with Derek Wyatt, the Labour MP, being quoted as saying: 'We have been campaigning against foxhunting, bearbaiting and cockfighting, and this is the human equivalent.'

Well now, Derek, that's not strictly true, is it? Ultimate fighters are not sitting at home with Mrs Fox and the babies, Foxy and Woxy, when a bunch of snarling dogs come bursting through the front door. Nobody is forcing them into the cage. And they are not kids from sink estates either. There are three British fighters; one has a degree in electronics from Kent University.

Even so, a spokesman for the British Medical Association said that it's a ghastly sport and that the point is to inflict injury on an opponent, which is wrong. No it isn't. If a man, of his own free will, wishes to get into a ring and spend half an hour being kicked and possibly eaten by another man, then what business is that of yours, mine or Derek Wyatt's?

I must say, at this juncture, that I don't like fighting. I prefer passive resistance and, if that doesn't work, active fleeing. Once a friend and I donned boxing gloves 'for a bit of a laugh' and pranced round each other making snarly faces. Then he hit me in the ear and I simply could not believe how much it hurt. 'Ow,' I said, in a rather unmanly way.

Then there was the time in Greece when a swarthy fisherman punched me in the face. So why didn't I hit him back? Well, this is hard to do when you are lying on your back in a dead faint.

Of course, the argument goes that war–war is the preserve of the intellectually stunted whereas the intellectually lofty prefer jaw–jaw. But consider this: I could have jawed with Stavros for hours and he still would have hit me.

Only last night, in the pub, I found myself in the middle of a huge argument. I was suggesting that the Israelis really had gone mad this time and that those shots of the tanks in Jenin were no different from the shots of German tanks in Warsaw. My opponent, on the other hand, was sympathetic to Ariel Sharon and felt his actions were justified in the face of endless Palestinian terrorism.

Neither of us was going to back down and so on we surged. The whole evening was swallowed by a tangle of twisted statistics, spurious historical fact and eventually, of course, that inevitable descent into a spume-filled barrel of finger-poking personal abuse.

That's the trouble with jaw—jaw. There can be no winner. You are forced to go on and on for ever. Or are you? Surely, if you want to make an adversary see things your way – and that's the whole point – then why not simply punch him?

Speaking with the benefit of experience, I assure you that if it were a choice of backing down from a firmly held conviction or being punched in the face again, I would back down and whimper like a dog.

I look sometimes at the politicians on *Question Time*, endlessly trotting out statistics and five-year plans in a desperate bid to make the adversary look like a fool. But why waste time? Let your opponent have his say, then hit him.

Certainly this would make the programme more interesting. Imagine it. Oliver Letwin delivers his piece on rising crime and how the Tories will get more bobbies on the beat. Then Stephen Byers leaps over his desk and kicks him. You would watch that, wouldn't you? I would.

I would especially like to see Edward Heath biting Denis Healey.

John Prescott has had a stab at it, literally, and his left

jab was widely regarded as the most interesting feature of the last general election campaign.

Every week, at the moment, David Dimbleby winds up *Question Time* by inviting people to get in touch if they want to be in the audience, but if we thought there was a chance of watching Ann Widdecombe pulling Glenda Jackson's hair, the producers would be beating willing spectators back with a stick.

There is something else, too. In the coming weeks Sharon and Yasser Arafat may meet around a table and talk about what can be done. They will conclude, after weeks and weeks, that there is no common ground and that in 50 years the Palestinians and the Israelis will still be blowing one another to pieces.

So here's a thought. Ariel and Yasser, one on one, in a cage at the Albert Hall. The winner gets Jerusalem.

Sunday 21 April 2002

Speaking As a Father, I'll Never be a Mother

Bob Geldof, perhaps the second most famous single dad in Britain, said last week that courts need to understand that not all men are brutal, indifferent boors who are incapable of raising children.

An interesting point, especially as it came on the same day as the result of an unusual custody battle in the Court of Appeal. Two parents, one a high-flying City executive on £300,000 a year, the other a full-time parent who gave up work in the early days of the marriage to look after the kids.

So who won? The one who gave up work? The one who's looked after them night and day for the past six years? Er, no. Even though it's the mother who works, it's the mother who won. The mother always wins.

Well not always, according to the lone parent group Gingerbread. It says that one in ten single parents is a man and that, clearly, courts do sometimes award residency orders to fathers. I'm sure they do, if the wife is a drooling vegetable, but I've never heard of it.

Indeed, the only two single fathers I know had the job thrust upon them because their wives died.

The fact of the matter is this. You, as a man, can put on your best suit and promise to read the children Harry Potter stories until dawn but you'll still lose. Even if your wife is sitting on the other side of the court wearing an 'I love Myra Hindley' T-shirt.

I think I know why. Last weekend I was entrusted with the task of being a single father for two days, and frankly I'd have been better off doing underwater knitting. I made a complete hash of it. When my wife arrived home on Sunday evening, way past the kids' bedtime, one child was bleeding profusely, one had left home and the other was stuck up a tree.

Things started to go wrong just after lunch on Saturday. They might have gone wrong before that but since I was locked in the office, writing, with *Led Zep II* on the stereo, it's hard to be sure.

Anyway, they went wrong after lunch because the dishwasher was full and I'm sorry, but I simply do not know how they work.

Oh, I can phase a DVD player so that six individual speakers can be made to come on and go off in whichever room I choose, but where do you put the salt in a dishwasher? And will any form of powder do? Well, not Coffee-mate, it turns out.

So what about washing machines? Nope. I can't work those either, and I've never seen the point of a deep-freeze since I only ever buy what I want now. Send me into a supermarket and I will emerge ten minutes later with a packet of Smarties and a copy of *GQ*. The notion of buying a pizza for the children's supper on Thursday simply wouldn't enter my head. So the need for a deep-freeze would never arise.

Am I alone with this white-goods phobia? I don't

think so. And I know for sure that I'm not the only man in the world who cannot cope.

It isn't that I won't. I can't. In the same way that I can't turn back time, or make a dishwasher wash dishes. I therefore had to get the six-year-old to wipe the three-year-old's bottom while I hid in a bush at the bottom of the garden.

Saturday night, I made a mistake. I knew that I'd have to get up at dawn, so did I get an early night? Was I grown up and womanly about things? No. What I did, in a manly way, was stay up half the night watching a television programme in which a group of twentysomething people, who were marooned on a desert island, stood on a log.

And then it was Sunday and everyone was clamouring for Sunday lunch, just like Mum makes. Impossible. Mums know, you see, what potato does what. Jersey Royal. Placenta previa. Maris piper. Lactate. These are Mum words.

I, on the other hand, had no clue that 'baking potatoes' – well that's what it said on the label – could also be used for roasting. So we had cauliflower instead and this, according to the seven-year-old, wasn't quite the same.

Clearing up wasn't quite the same either, because we didn't bother. Partly because the dishwasher was still unemptied and partly because I had some fairly big plans to build a den that afternoon. And this, I think, is the fundamental difference between men and women parents.

Had it been me coming home on a Sunday evening

after a weekend away, I'd have been greeted by three children in their pyjamas, washed, scrubbed, deloused and with their homework done. The pots would have been cleaned and the playroom would have gleamed like a pathology lab.

But I'd sort of glossed over the boring bits, or made a mess of them, and concentrated on teaching my six-year-old how to drive round the paddock on my new off-road go-kart, which is strictly not to be used by under-sixteens. We'd built a tree house, done joy rides on the old tractor, fallen over a lot, had a water fight and all fallen out.

To fathers, kids are fun. To mothers, they're a responsibility. That's why it's so important to have both. And it's also why, if there's no option, courts have to side with the mums.

Sunday 28 April 2002

I'm Just Talkin' 'Bout My Generation, Britney

He was in a band famous for singing the line 'Hope I die before I get old'. And now he has. John Entwistle may have been the quiet one, standing at the back while Roger Daltrey and Pete Townshend made merry up front, but anyone who knows The Who knows he was probably the only bassist in the world who could have kept up with the manic Keith Moon, a man who rightly called himself 'the best Keith Moon-style drummer in the world'.

More than that, if you listen to 'The Real Me' on *Quadrophenia*, Entwistle uses the bass to create a melody. And he wrote 'My Wife', which is one of the best tracks on one of the best albums from probably the best band the world has ever seen.

The Who were about to embark on a tour of America. It would have been a sell-out. That's because they were old, they'd been round the block and they knew what they were doing.

Every week Steve Wright hosts a round-table discussion on Radio 2 where people as famous as Peter Stringfellow come in to talk about the week's new releases. Usually they're absolute rubbish, an endless succession of teenagers reedily singing along to the background accompaniment of what sounds like a mobile-phone ring tone.

Take Britney Spears as a prime example. Occasionally you hear what is obviously her own voice but for the most part it's a computer interpretation and, as a result, it sounds as if she's coming at you via an answering machine.

What about Mary J. Blige, about whom everyone seems to be raving. Frankly, I'd rather listen to a pneumatic drill. She's nothing more than a spelling mistake – it should be Mary J. Bilge.

However, the other day they played a song that was spellbinding. 'At last,' I thought, 'here we have a new talent that can actually sing and a new song that's going somewhere.' But I was wrong. The song was 'Morning Dew' – which is old – and the vocalist was Robert Plant, Led Zeppelin's gnarled and wizened front man.

Admitting that I prefer Plant to Mary J. Bilge is probably not allowed these days, any more than it's allowed to say that you prefer the Conservative Party to His Tonyness. Certainly I know that I'm not allowed to say I went all the way to Wembley last week to see Roger Waters, the former Pink Floydist.

Indeed, lots of people asked where I was going on Wednesday night and I couldn't bring myself to tell the truth. 'I'm doing some canvassing for the BNP in Burnley' would have sounded better. 'I shall be downloading pornography from the internet' or 'I'm going to kill a fox'. Anything except saying I had tickets to see the anorak's anorak.

But do you know, it was brilliant. Brilliant and properly loud. Rick Mason, as he was called in the *Evening Standard*'s glowing review, guested on 'Set the Controls for the Heart of the Sun', while Snowy White and Andy Fairweather-Low gave it their all on the six strings. There was even a drum solo.

Best of all, the songs were long, which meant they had time to breathe. There was a beginning, a fifteen-minute crescendo in the middle and a gradual descent to the end. What's wrong with that? Who says songs have to be fast? – not Mozart, that's for sure.

I'm sorry to bang on about the Slow Food movement again but most people seem to think it's a good idea. These guys have decided that Europe should be defined by long lunches and that the American sandwich is nothing more than fuel for the devil.

They want to see towns full of coffee shops and squares full of people passing the time of day with one another, not rushing off to make another phone call. For them, Vesta is the Antichrist, and they are getting enormous support. Most people like the idea of small shops selling high-quality local produce, even if the queue stretches out of the door and it takes a week to be served.

Yes, a supermarket is convenient and a Big Mac hits the spot when you're in a hurry but why does music have to be this way? Why is three minutes acceptable and twenty minutes pretentious? Would 'Stairway to Heaven' be improved if they cut out the bustle in its hedgerow? I think not.

They say that radio stations prefer short songs and that

Bo' Rap, as Ben Elton calls it, simply wouldn't get any airplay if it were released today, but I can't for the life of me work out why. Jimmy Young's an old man these days and there's no way he could get from his studio to the lavatory and back before Britney was over. He needs a scaramouche in his fandango if he's to stand a chance.

Maybe it's an attention-span thing. Music is now the backdrop to our lives rather than an event in itself. We put on a CD while we're doing something else. I can't remember the last time I put on an album and listened to it in a chair with my eyes closed.

I shall be doing just that today, however. If you're in Chipping Norton and you hear a strange noise, it'll be me listening to 'Won't Get Fooled Again'. And I won't be, either. I like 1970s rock music and I'm not ashamed to admit it.

Sunday 30 June 2002

Chin Up, My Little Angel – Winning is for Losers

My eldest daughter is not sleek. In fact, to be brutally honest she has the aerodynamic properties of a bungalow and the coordination of an American bombing raid.

She puts a huge effort into running. Her arms and legs flail around like the Flying Scotsman's pistons but despite this you need a theodolite to ascertain that she is actually moving forwards. She's a bit of a duffer at the school's sports day.

Luckily, the school tries to operate a strict 'no competition' rule. The game starts, children exert energy and then the game finishes. This doesn't work terribly well with the 50-metre running race but often there are never any winners and consequently there are never any losers.

That's the theory, but round the edge of the sports ground there's a communal picnic for parents. I had been asked to bring along a potato salad, which sounds simple enough but oh no. My potato salad was going to be creamier and made with higher-quality potatoes than anyone else's potato salad. This is why I got up at 4.30 a.m. to make it.

Nobody was going to scoop my potato salad quietly into the bushes. Nobody was going to make joke retching noises behind my back. I was out there to win, to crush the competition like beetles.

My daughter did not understand. 'You told me it doesn't matter if I come last in the race,' she said.

'It doesn't,' I replied.

'So why,' she pressed on, 'are you trying to win a competition for potato salads when there isn't one?'

There bloody well was. And a competition for pasta salads, too. And quiche. But all of these paled alongside the brownie wars.

Obviously, I chose the ones made by my wife but pretty soon I was surrounded by a gaggle of women. 'Try mine,' they said. 'Try mine.' It was just like the old days when schools had teams and competition and everyone crowded round shouting: 'Pick me, pick me.'

I was never picked. I was always left at the back like the spring onion in the bottom of the fridge: 'Oh do we have to have Clarkson, sir? He's useless.'

I was therefore determined that no brownie should be left out, but this wasn't enough. I was being pushed to decide, publicly, whose was best: my wife's with the creamy centre; the ones made with chocolate that had been specially imported from America; or the ones with pecans floating in the middle. 'They were all lovely,' I said, sticking to the spirit of the day.

What spirit? What's the point of protecting children from the horror of failure on the sports pitch when their parents are all giving one another Chinese burns on the touchline? 'My brownies are better than yours. Say it! Say it!'

I spoke last night to a man who bunged one of the teachers 50 quid at his daughter's sports day, saying:

'Look, if it's close for first and second, you know what to do.'

The following year his daughter wrote to him saying: 'Dear Dad, please let me come where I come. Don't try to bribe anyone.' He did as asked and she came in second. But he wasn't finished. He took the cup she won to the engravers and had it inscribed with a big '1st'.

It's not as if children don't understand the concept of losing. Mine regularly have their stomachs blown open by aliens or their heads kicked in by a Russian agent.

Of course, you could be good parents and turn up at sports day with a bowl of tinned prunes. You could force your children to put the PlayStation away and stick to Monopoly, which has no winners and losers because nobody in the whole of human history has ever had the patience to finish a game.

Think about it. If your child has no understanding of failure, how will he cope when he walks round the back of the bike sheds one day to find his girlfriend in a passionate embrace with Miggins Major? There'll be a bloodbath.

I don't want my children to be unhappy. Ever. It broke my heart when, as predicted, Emily was last in her running race, thumping across the line like a buffalo. I couldn't bear to watch her fighting back the tears of humiliation.

But what do you do? Well, why not teach them that losing is better than winning. Certainly, it's impossible to make someone laugh if you've come home first. 'So anyway, I got the deal, won the lottery and woke up in bed the next day with Cameron Diaz and Claudia Schiffer.' That's nice but it's not funny.

Furthermore, arranging your face when you win is impossible. You have to look proud but magnanimous and that's hard even for Dustin Hoffman. Michael Schumacher has been winning since he was eight and he still can't pull it off.

All the funniest people in life are abject and total failures. There's no such thing as a funny supermodel or a successful businessman who causes your sides to split every time he opens his mouth.

This is presumably why I felt a certain sense of pride as we trudged home from the sports day picnic. Everyone else was carrying empty bowls that had been licked clean. And me? Well, my bowl was still full of uneaten potato salad.

And I got a column out of it.

Sunday 7 July 2002

A Murderous Fox Has Made Me Shoot David Beckham

Let's be perfectly clear, shall we. The fox is not a little orange puppy dog with doe eyes and a waggly tail. It's a disease-ridden wolf with the morals of a psychopath and the teeth of a great white shark.

Only last month a foxy-woxy broke into someone's council house and tried to eat a baby. I'm not joking. The poor child's parents found their son's face being mauled by one of these monsters as he slept on the sofa. And worse, I woke up last Tuesday to find a fox had pulled Michael Owen's head off. For fun.

Perhaps I should explain at this point that Michael Owen is one of our new chickens, which were bought, and it pains me to say this, because stuff from the garden does taste better than stuff from the shop. Even to a man who can't tell fish from cheese. If I could, they'd get rid of Mr Dyslexia and let me do the restaurant reviews as well.

Certainly, I need the extra money to pay for my new-found organic love affair. Pigeons have eaten all my sweet peas, scale insect has infested my tomatoes and now Michael Owen has been decapitated.

The children were hysterical and blamed me for not buying a secure henhouse. Obviously, I tried to convince them it was all Tony Blair's fault, but it was no good.

So I had to spend £150 on a hut that looks like Fort Knox, and a further £100 on a cage for the hens to run around in.

The next morning we skipped down the garden like something out of *The Railway Children*. We knew Daddy would be on the train and that everything would be rosy. But it wasn't.

Sol Campbell was gone and finding out how this had happened did not require much in the way of detective work. My garden looked like Stalag Luft III after Charles Bronson had been let loose with the gardening tools. One of the tunnels, I swear, ended up in Burton upon Trent.

Even I was angry, so that afternoon I went to one of those spy shops in London and blew £350 on a pair of infrared night-vision goggles. Unfortunately they were made in Russia, which is another way of saying: 'Made badly by someone who's drunk.' So they don't work very well.

At close range they're fine, but at anything more than three or four inches everything's just a blur. Certainly, if this is the best Russia can come up with now, we really didn't have anything to worry about in the Cold War. Its tanks would have ended up in Turkey after its air force had spent the night bombing the bejesus out of the Irish Sea.

However, if you concentrate hard you can just tell what's an organic life form and what's a stone mushroom. And so, as the last vestiges of sunlight faded from the western horizon and the sky went black, I was to be found at my bedroom window with a 12-bore Beretta at my side. Foxy-Woxy was going to die.

By one in the morning I'd nearly polished off a bottle of Brouilly and it was becoming increasingly hard to figure out what was what in the green world of infrared. But, yes, I was pretty sure there was a glow in the garden where before all had been dark.

I made a mental, if slightly drunken, calculation about where this was in relation to various trees, before putting the night-vision goggles down, picking up the piece and firing.

The next morning my wife was distressed to find that her Scotts of Stow chair had been blown to smithereens. And I'm afraid she could not be persuaded that through night-vision goggles it had looked like a fox. 'Maybe through beer goggles,' she said.

So the next night I was forced to stake out the garden sober. This meant I was still awake and alert at three when I noticed movement by the cage. I raised the gun and once again the serenity of the still night air was shattered as the weapon spat a hail of lead.

Over breakfast the next day there was a scream from down the garden. 'You f★★★★★★ idiot. You've shot David Beckham.' And I had. I tried hard to convince the children that she'd been savaged by vermin but it was no good. Luckily for the world's police forces, there's a big difference between a gunshot wound and a fox attack.

So now I've been banned from late-night sentry duty and I'm stuck. I can't put poison down because the dogs will eat it. And I can't use the dogs to get the fox because Mr Blair will be angry. What's more, I can't simply let nature take its course, because then all my hens will be killed and we'll end up eating supermarket eggs and dying of salmonella, listeria or whatever it is they say will kill us this week.

This is what the metropolitan elite don't understand: that the countryside is a complicated place and that pretty soon they won't be able to buy organic nut loaf because a bunch of foxes will have held up the delivery truck and eaten its contents long before it reaches Hoxton.

The simple fact of the matter is this. I've tried to do my bit. I've tried to become organic. And all I have to show for it is a cockerel called Nicky Butt and a hen called David Seaman.

Sunday 14 July 2002

I Bring You News from the Edge of the Universe

For me, there is no greater pleasure than lying on my back in the middle of a deep, black desert, staring at the night sky. I simply love having my mind boggled by the enormity of the numbers: the fact we're screaming around the sun at 90 miles a second, and the sun is careering around the universe at a million miles a day.

Then there's the notion that one of those stars up there could have ceased to exist a thousand years ago. Yet we're still seeing its light.

Best of all, though, is that we're about 3,000 light years from the edge of our galaxy – that's 17,600,000,000,000,000 miles. And yet, on a clear night near Tucson once, I saw it. I actually saw it, and that was, please believe me, utterly breathtaking.

I therefore quite understand why people are drawn to the science of astronomy. Certainly, I'm not surprised that after 40 years of fumbling around, quite literally, in the dark, Britain's astronomers have just handed over £80 million and joined forces with the Europeans.

This means they now have access to the VLT (which stands for Very Large Telescope) at the ESO (which stands for European Southern Observatory) in Chile. They will also help build the OWL (which stands for OverWhelmingly Large telescope). And, boy, with all these snappy acronyms, can't you just tell this is basically a GO. Which stands for German Operation.

But let's be honest, since Galileo disproved the Old Testament, astronomers have simply been dotting the 'i's and crossing the 't's. Only last month, a meteorite shaved half an inch of ozone from the Earth's atmosphere, and did they see it coming? Did they hell as like.

Occasionally, they show us a photograph of some cosmic explosion. But bangs without the bang never seem to work somehow. Remember: in space, nobody can hear you scream.

What's more, I need scale. I need something to be the size of a 'double-decker bus' or a 'football pitch' before I get the point. Tell me that they're burning 20,000 square kilometres of rainforest every day and I won't care. Tell me that they're burning an area the size of Wales and I still won't care, but I'll understand what you're on about.

I'm afraid then that a photograph of Alpha 48///bB1 blowing itself to smithereens may be pretty, but getting access to the camera cost £80 million, and that seems excessive.

So, what about the question of extraterrestrial life?

Hollywood has convinced us that the night sky is full of aliens watching *Holby City*. But the reality is less romantic. The Seti organisation, which searches for life in the universe, and which was immortalised by Jodie Foster's film *Contact*, has spent £95 million and seventeen years listening to the night skies. And it has found absolutely nothing.

However, let's say it does. Let's say that one day some computer geek actually picks up Corillian FM and let's say we get a message back to them along the lines of 'Yoo hoo'.

Then what? At worst, the Corillians will beam themselves to Earth and eat all our family pets. 'Hmm, Labrador – nice with watercress.' And at best, they will invite us over for drinks. Sounds good, but how do you suppose we will get there?

The space shuttle can only do 17,500 mph, which is pretty fast in Earth terms, but for getting around the galaxy you may as well get out and walk. At 17,500 mph it would take 29 years for the shuttle to get out of our own solar system which, in cosmic terms, is about as far as your front door.

To stand even the remotest chance of getting to wherever you're going before the crew dies, you need light speed. But here too there's a problem – the faster you go, the more time slows down. This is a scientific fact. I spend my life driving quickly, which is why I have a 1970s haircut.

So, if you could build something that did 186,000 miles a second, you would be out of the solar system in 6 hours. But you'd end up in 1934.

Certainly, you'd arrive before the decision was made to send you. Worse, you'd arrive before the Corillians sent their invite and this would be social death.

Really, we know for a fact that humankind will never be able to travel at the speed of light because to do so would mean travelling backwards in time. And this, in turn, means our world of today would be full of people from the future. People would end up marrying their own grandchildren. It would be a mess.

Let's summarise then. Astronomers spend their time lying on their backs looking at stars, but what's the point? They can't spot meteorites that are on a collision course with Earth, and even if they could, would we want to know? And if they do find life out there, we will never be able to pop over and say 'Hi'.

However, I fully support this £80-million investment. Because if a sixteenth-century astronomer using a tiny telescope was able to prove the Bible wrong, think what damage could be inflicted by today's astronomers with their VLTs and their OWLs on the nonsense science of astrology. Just £80 million to make a mockery of Russell Grant – I'll have some of that.

Sunday 21 July 2002

Go to the Big Top: It's Better than *Big Brother*

What on earth are you all doing in the evening these days? I see television viewing figures so I know you're not in front of the box and I also know, because pubs are closing down at the rate of one a day, that you're not in the boozer.

You can't all have Sony PlayStations, so new technology isn't the answer, and obviously you aren't at the theatre or there would be no need for Arts Council grants.

I thought perhaps you might all be out dancing but I read in the papers last week that Cream, the rave club in Liverpool, has seen attendances quartered in the past ten years. Judging by the pitiful sales of books these days, you're not curled up in front of the fire reading.

In fact, if you add up the officially produced numbers of people who do the usual stuff in the evening – drinking, cinema, theatre, eating out, watching television, having sex and reading – you are left with an eerie conclusion. Every night twenty million people do absolutely nothing.

This week I became one of 'the disappeared'. First of all I am still largely preoccupied with finding and murdering the fox that's killing my chickens and second I went to the circus. And neither, thanks to various animal rights organisations such as Born Free, the RSPCA and the Labour Party, are listed as officially recognised pastimes.

I'm dimly aware of having enjoyed traditional big-top circuses when I was little, apart from the clowns, who were downright scary, but I'm also dimly aware that such circuses were sort of outcast a couple of years ago when Mary Chipperfield was found guilty of being rude to a monkey.

I think this was probably sensible. I don't normally agree with the RSPCA since I believe it is the duty of an animal to be on my plate at supper time but, that said, it's hard to condone wanton cruelty.

And circuses were cruel. They had boxing kangaroos that were plainly off their heads, and animal-rights activists were forever opening up cages to find that the elephants had eaten their own dung and the tigers had bitten off their own tails. If they'd given a fox some cannabis and told it to jump through hoops of fire, that would have been fine. Foxes deserve to be humiliated. But there's something hideous about watching a lion, the king of the jungle, standing on one leg in a tutu.

There was something equally hideous about the 'modern' circus which replaced the Chipperfield original. This usually involved a message of some kind and the message was usually about Margaret Thatcher: 'Next up tonight, ladies and gentlemen, Dave Spart, who will use mime to explain the relationship between poll tax and apartheid.'

Not exactly family entertainment, and nor were the

French and Canadian alternatives, which tended to feature dwarfs juggling chainsaws.

It really did look, as the new millennium dawned, as if the circus had been buried for good. Even the Dome, which was the biggest top of them all, reinforced that. So what was I doing in a tent last week?

I have no idea but I can tell you that, as live entertainment goes, it blew Darcy Bussell into the hedgerow and the Rolling Stones into the middle of last week.

It was called Gifford's Circus and it was held in a tent of a size that would be familiar to anyone who has camped out on Everest. There were no clowns in terrifying suits and they had not plundered the Kalahari for animals. In fact the only four-legged entertainment came right at the end when a dog, belonging to someone in the audience, sauntered into the ring and got its lipstick out. It was that kind of show.

They had two jugglers from Ethiopia, who are apparently on the verge of taking a world record with their back-to-back routine. And they had Ralph and Celia, who came on in Victorian bathing costumes and played what appeared to be a game of aerial twister. Did you know it was possible to stand on one leg with a woman balanced on your nose? No, I didn't either.

I don't want to sound like some tweedy duffer who thinks television is the devil's eye, but there was something uplifting about this simple rural entertainment. Believe me, watching a man taking off his trousers on a tightrope is amazing. I can't even do it in a bedroom without falling over. It was uplifting because it was so 'up close and personal', and so small and so low-budget that you could see there was no computerised trickery.

Isn't that what you want from entertainment – seeing people do things you cannot do yourself? *Big Brother*? Give me the big top any day. If you are one of the twenty million dispossessed who stare at a wall every night because you can't think of anything better to do, give the local circus a try. I think you'll like it.

I was going to finish up at this point with something edgy and sharp. Something a little bit cool and now. But in the spirit of the piece I will leave you with this:

A goat goes into a jobcentre and asks in perfect English for some work. The slightly amazed clerk has a look through his files and says he could try the circus.

'The circus?' says the goat. 'Why would the circus want a bricklayer?'

Sunday 28 July 2002

The Nit-picking Twitchers Out to Ground Britain

House prices are teetering on the edge of a bottomless hole and pretty soon anything with less than six or seven bedrooms will be worth less than its contents.

There's a very good reason for this. As far as I can tell, every single house in Britain is on the flight path for one of the government's proposed new airports. No village is exempt. No dale is deemed too beautiful. No town is too small or inconsequential. Even Rugby, apparently, needs four runways, six terminals and 5,000 miles of chain-link fencing. Nottingham, too, and Exeter – everywhere does.

The thinking behind this is worryingly simple. The government, fresh from its success with the Millennium Dome and the River of Fire, has worked out that no people in Britain flew on commercial airlines in 1901 and 180 million did in 2001. So, using the same sort of maths that brought us Gordon Brown's shiny new overdraft, it reckons 500 million people will be landing and taking off from British airports in 2030.

That's half the population of China. It's twice the population of America. It's everyone in Britain using a plane ten times a year. And that seems unlikely somehow.

Still, if you reckon half a billion people will be needing

a runway within 28 years, it's easy to understand why every field in the land is currently earmarked as a potential airport.

This has led to a biblical outbreak of Nimbyism. Councils affected by the proposal to build a massive new airport on the Kent marshes took the government to court last week, saying the extra noise should go to Gatwick. So now, we can be sure, the people of Sussex will be fighting back.

This will turn Tunbridge Wells into the West Bank. It'll be father versus son, mother versus daughter, neighbour versus neighbour. And it will all be completely pointless because, let me explain right now, there is no way in hell that an airport will ever be built on the Medway marshes.

First of all, since London swelled up to the size of Belgium, Kent is as inaccessible as the South Pole or Mars. Given the choice of going on holiday via an airport in the middle of the Thames estuary or staying at home and beating myself over the head with a brick, I'd stay at home.

Of course, they could get round this by building better road and rail links but what they could never get round is the most fearsome organisation in the entire world. In a straight battle between this lot and Al-Qaeda, Osama bin Laden would end up killing himself to escape from the hounding. It can nit-pick a man to death from 400 paces. It never gives up. Its members are terminators. Ladies and gentlemen, I give you . . . the Royal Society for the Protection of Birds.

The twitchers have pointed out that the Medway marshes are home to the country's largest heronry and that is pretty much that. A simple avocet would have done the trick but they've come up with a whole herd of herons so one thing's for sure; there will be no Kent airport.

A couple of weeks ago I wrote about some environmental protesters in China who had wheeled out a dolphin to try to stop the massive Yangtze dam. And Chinese officials had got round the problem by shooting it.

But that will never happen here. The mere fact that we have this consultation shows how democratic we've become. Now everyone has the chance to object. As a result, nothing will happen until the end of time. No matter where the government selects, there will always be a slug or a beetle or a butterfly.

What we need at a time like this is someone who can machete their way through the eco-twaddle. We need someone who can shove the government's projections back up Alistair Darling's new hole czar. We need a realist at the helm. And I can think of nobody better qualified than me.

Video conferencing and emails take up less time and involve less risk for businessmen than being chased across the Atlantic by heat-seeking missiles. So I can see, in the fullness of time, a dramatic fall in the demand for business travel.

However, there will be a significant increase in the number of people travelling for fun. And, as I said earlier, it won't be fun if they have to set off from a mudflat on the Medway or a business park in Rugby.

You have to leave via London and – contrary to the claims made by Stansted, which is in Bishop's Stortford, or Gatwick, which is in Brighton – the capital has only one airport: Heathrow.

The government's proposals seem to call for one new short runway but what good is that? Build six new long ones and be done with it. They will be able to handle the bigger planes that are coming. Heathrow is more accessible than any other airport in Britain and nobody living nearby can complain because it was there before they were. They're all deaf anyway but six planes landing at once are not six times louder than six planes landing one at a time.

However, best of all, the RSPB can't object because any birds native to the reservoirs of Staines were long since sucked into the Trent engine of a passing 777 and shredded.

Sunday 1 December 2002

Cricket's the National Sport of Time Wasters

I understand that England recently lost a game of cricket. Good. The more we lose, the more our interest in the game wanes and the less it will dominate our newspapers and television screens.

Cricket – and I will not take any argument – is boring. Any sport which goes on for so long that you might need a 'comfort break' is not a sport at all. It is merely a means of passing the time. Like reading.

Of course, we used to have televised reading. It was called *Jackanory*. Now we have *Buffy the Vampire Slayer*, which is much better. Things have moved on, but cricket has not.

I'm not sure that it can. Even if Nasser Hussain, who is the captain of England, were to invest in some new hair and marry Council House Spice (aka Claire Sweeney, the ex-*Brookside* actress turned *Big Brother* contestant), it wouldn't make any difference.

Nobody is quite sure how cricket began, though many people believe it was invented by shepherds who used their crooks to defend the wicket gate to the sheep fold. This would certainly figure because shepherds had many long hours to while away, with nothing much to do.

The first written reference to cricket was in 1300, when Prince Edward played it with his friend Piers

Gaveston. And again, this would figure. Princes, in those days, were not exactly rushed off their feet.

Cricket was spread around the world by British soldiers who found themselves marooned in godforsaken flea-bitten parts of the world and needed something to keep them amused, not just for an hour but for week after interminable week.

Today Australia dominates the game – which furthers my theory. Of course they're good at it. They have no distractions. And the only way we can ever beat them is to round up the unemployed and the wastrels and give them all bats. Certainly, they'd feel at home in the pavilion. It's exactly the same as sitting in a bus shelter all day.

Let me put it this way – is there a sound more terrifying on a Sunday afternoon than a child saying: 'Daddy. Can we play Monopoly?'

Like cricket, Monopoly has no end. The rules explain how you can unmortgage a property and when you should build hotels on Bond Street but they don't say, and they should, that the winner is the last player left alive. And what about Risk? You make a calculation, based on the law of averages, that you can take the world but you're always stymied by the law of probability and end up out of steam, throwing an endless succession of twos and ones in Kamchatka. Still, this is preferable to the modern version in which George W. Bush invades Iraq and we all die of smallpox.

Happily, my children are now eight, six and four so they're way past the age when board games hold any appeal. Given the choice of mortgaging Old Kent Road or shooting James Bond on a PlayStation, they'll take the electronic option every time.

Then there are jigsaws, which I once had to explain to a Greek. 'Yes, you spend a couple of weeks putting all the pieces together so you end up with a picture.'

'Then what happens?' he asked.

'Well, you break it up again and put it back in the box.'

It's not often I've felt empathy with a Greek, but I did then. And it's much the same story with crosswords. If scientists could harness the brainpower spent every day on trying to find the answer to 'Russian banana goes backwards in France we hear perhaps', then maybe mankind might have cured cancer by now.

Crosswords, like jigsaws and cricket, are not really games in themselves. They are simply tools for wasting time. And that's not something that sits well in the modern world.

We may dream of living the slow life, taking a couple of hours over lunch and eating cheese until dawn, but the reality is that we have a heart attack if the traffic lights stay red for too long or the lift doors fail to close the instant we're ready to go.

Answering-machine messages are my particular bugbear. I want a name and a number, and that's it. I don't have time to sit and listen to where you'll be at three and who you'll be seeing and why you need to talk before then. And even if I do pick up the phone personally, I don't want a chat. I'm a man. I don't do chatting. Say what you have to say and go away.

British film-makers still haven't got this. They spend hours with their sepia lighting and their long character-developing speeches and it's all pointless because we'd much rather watch a muscly American saying: 'Die, m***********r.'

Slow-cooked lamb shanks for supper? Oh for God's sake, I'll get a takeaway.

Cricket, then, is from a bygone age when people invested their money in time rather than in things. And now we have so many things to play with and do, it seems odd to waste it watching somebody else playing what's basically an elaborate game of catch.

Please stop watching – then it will go away.

Sunday 8 December 2002

Have I Got News . . . I'm Another Failed Deayton

Over the years I've always said no to appearing on *Have I Got News For You*. Actually, that's not true. I haven't always said no, because they only asked once. However, had they asked again, I would have said no again.

There didn't seem to be any upside. I would sit there, dripping like cheese in an old sock, while Ian Hislop, Paul Merton and Angus Deayton skated elegantly around their carefully choreographed and heavily scripted routine.

Like pretty well everyone, I knew how the show was put together. Throughout the week, a room full of the brightest writers in the land would crank out jokes and then on studio day the presenters would hone and perm them to perfection.

The guests? Well they'd be like snotty kids, strapping themselves into a Spitfire and going up there, alone, against an entire battle-hardened German squadron. Yes, they might fire off a few bullets but they'd end up full of holes.

However, when the call came through a couple of weeks ago to sit in the main chair, I needed smelling salts. 'What, be the quizmaster? Me – the car bloke?'

This was like being asked to run the state opening of

parliament. I'd have the team on my side, making sure the throne was gold enough and that my crown wouldn't fall off. 'Yes. Just yes.'

It was a bit disappointing that the evening before I was due to record I had been invited to go out with four jolly attractive women who'd spent the previous few weeks learning how to be strippers and who needed a man to accompany them on a tour of London's lap-dancing venues.

Normally, the Four Horsemen of the Apocalypse couldn't have dragged me from that opportunity. But attempting to fly on *HIGNFY* with a hangover and no sleep was not sensible, so I was in bed at 11 o'clock in my smart pyjamas with the bunny rabbit ears.

In the morning a motorcyclist brought round the finished script on a purple cushion. It was very, very funny. And apparently quite simple, too. I just had to sit there, waiting for Paul and Ian to finish their prepared verbal tennis, then I would read my gags from the autocue, pick up the cheque (with a forklift truck) and go home.

Er, well, it's not quite like that.

I arrived at the studios at 9.30 in the morning to find that Geoffrey Robinson, the former paymaster-general, had been charged with a selection of motoring offences. Plainly, this was good material. So half the script was thrown away to make room, and then the trouble started.

Obviously the three scriptwriters, headed by snake-hipped Jed, wanted to dwell on the white powder that had allegedly been found in Robinson's car,* but the lawyers said it would be better to call it a substance. A substance? That was no good. A substance could be something on the bottom of his shoe. So after an hour or so everyone agreed that it could be called a 'mystery powder'.

So where were Paul and Ian while this was going on? Well, to be blunt, they were at home, in loose robes. They didn't breeze in till six. And do you know something? They had not seen a script; they didn't even know who the guests were.

All they see before the show, and I mean half an hour before the tape-players start to turn, are the photographs to which they are asked to come up with captions and the four people in the odd-one-out round. They had the same amount of preparation as the guests.

Let me tell you something else, too. I had always imagined that after twelve years of being professionally cynical they would be cruel and bitter and combative.

But they were like parents before a school sports day. 'Don't worry,' they kept saying, 'do your best. It's not the winning.' They were so kind that they nearly managed to shut down the hydrants in my armpits.

And God they're quick. I would ask a question that I know they had never seen or heard before and they'd be off, with a top-of-the-head banter that left me breathless. I wish you could have seen the full hour and

---

* These allegations later proved to be completely unfounded, and no charges were ever brought.

40 minutes that they recorded rather than just the 29 minutes that was transmitted.

I'm sorry to sound so gushing but Paul is properly funny. And crammed into that tiny head, Ian has an encyclopaedia.

I should explain that they really do care about winning. Which is odd because, from where I was sitting, the scores seemed to mount up in an entirely arbitrary fashion. I have no idea why Paul ended up with sixteen and Ian with eleven. So far as I could work out, they both got nought.

And me? Well, I spent most of the evening reading from the autocue when I should have been looking at the notes on my desk. I forgot to ask two questions completely, I lost my earpiece so I couldn't hear the instructions from the gallery and at no point did I ever know who was supposed to be answering what.

Doubtless it will all have looked seamless on television – they even managed to make sense of Boris Johnson. But the simple fact of the matter is that 7 million people will have watched my performance and thought: 'Nope. He wasn't as good as Angus Deayton either.'

I agree. And nobody ever will be.

Sunday 22 December 2002

Home Alone Can be the Perfect State for a Child

Just last week I left my children, aged eight, six and four, at home alone. I only needed to buy the papers and it was just too much of a faff to find all their shoes and get them in the car when I'd only be gone, at most, for five minutes.

Of course I was in a total panic about it. Sure, I'd asked the neighbour to keep an ear out, I'd written down my mobile phone number and I'd explained where the gun was, and how it could be speed-loaded should someone unsavoury come to the door.

But despite these extensive precautions I still came back expecting to find them either in the fire or in white slavery in Turkmenistan.

So, like everyone else, I was horrified to learn this week that two mothers had left their kids at home while they went off, not for the papers, but for a holiday.

One woman had arrived at Manchester airport where she found her son needed a passport (yeah, right), so she'd put him in a taxi and sent him home. The other had gone skiing. Dreadful. What's the world coming to? Something must be done.

However, let's stop and think for a moment. The children left behind were eleven and twelve and, while this may seem young to those of us of a forty-ish disposition, we have to face the fact that today eleven is the new seventeen.

If I'd been left at home alone when I was eleven, I'd have been dead of hunger or electrocution within the hour. Come to think of it, if I were left at home aged 42 there'd be the same result in the same sort of time frame.

We might like to think of an eleven-year-old as some newborn foal, all slimy and incapable with wobbly legs, but it's not that long ago that eleven-year-olds were skilled in the arts of mining and pickpocketry. And nothing's changed.

Today, most eleven-year-olds can make a roach, hot-wire a car, outrun the police, fight an entire army of aliens, drink a bottle of vodka without being sick and operate a digital satellite transceiver. So they should have no trouble at all with a microwave and a tin opener.

Certainly, most eleven-year-olds are far better able to fend for themselves than most eighty-year-olds. And the state has no qualms about leaving them all by themselves for week after interminable week with no pension and no reliable means of reaching the lavatory on time.

Can an eighty-year-old program a television or under-stand packet food? Can an eighty-year-old afford the heating bills? Not usually.

Of course an eleven-year-old cannot afford heating bills either but at least he can hack into the power company's accounts and adjust his bill to nought.

Furthermore, you should put yourself in the shoes of the eleven-year-old. At home. Alone. Over Christmas.

For an eighty-year-old this is hell on earth, but for an eleven-year-old it's about as close to heaven as you can get while your heart is still beating.

No hirsute old ladies queuing up to kiss you on the mouth. No Queen's broadcast to the nation.

No sprouts. No Boxing Day parties with people 'from the village', no need to wait until Christmas morning to play with your new Xbox game, and no need to worry that someone might want to watch television instead.

No need to open presents which you know are jumpers. No being dragged off to church on Christmas Eve. Put your feet on the furniture, dig out Mum's X-rated videos, wonder who Joe Strummer was and set the garage to loud.

And because you can eat what you want, where you want, with your fingers, while slouching, and with your elbows on the table, there will be no family rows and no volcanic explosions as, for the only time in a whole year, a family is forced to coexist in a small space for a long time.

I don't want to be bah-humbug about this. I love the idea of a Christmas around the tree, watching my children unwrap their presents and settling down after lunch to watch Steve McQueen on his motorcycle. But those days are gone and they won't be back.

Let's not forget that today is the past that people in the future will dream about.

The fact is that I'm with my children for a maximum of fifteen minutes a day, and this is no match for the constant bombardment they get on Radio 1 from Sara

Cox and the Cheeky Girls. I want my eight-year-old to be a good girl. But over Christmas I learn she wants to be a 'teenage dirtbag baby'.

So, I suspect the mother who goes to Spain over Christmas without her bolshie, prepubescent, mono-syllabic, baggy-trousered son will have a better time as a result. But maybe the boy would, too.

Of course, giving independence to the pre-teens may sound sad, horrific even, like a return to Dickensian times. But if we accept they're capable and socially active at ten or eleven, it might also get the government out of a hole. Because while the state may be unable to afford to pay pensions, parents could get support from their children by sending the ungrateful, mollycoddled spoilt little brats up some chimneys.

Sunday 29 December 2002

Ivan the Terrible is One Hell of a Holidaymaker

A recent survey found that the British are the most hated of all the world's holidaymakers, but to be honest it's hard to see why.

For sure, a group of electricians from Rochdale on holiday in Ibiza might be a bit noisy, and they may be sick on the municipal flowerbeds from time to time, but us – you and me – in our rented farmhouses in Provence, we're no bother at all. We eat the local cheese. We drink the local wine. We say '*bonsoir*' to the postman every morning. We're as good as gold.

The Germans, on the other hand, make terrible bed-fellows. Mainly because when they're around there are no beds left. Ever since we were introduced, socially, by package holidays in the 1960s, we've known that when it comes to antisocial buffet-hogging pigheadedness on holiday, the Germans are in a class of their own.

But not any more. I've just come back from Dubai, where I spent some time at Wild Wad, an enormous water park where you sit on the inner tube from a tractor and then get knocked off it in 101 new and exciting ways you'd never thought of.

There were, as you can imagine, fairly long queues for the better rides, but hey, that's okay. We could handle the wait. We're patient. We're British. And that means we're the best queuers in the whole world.

Oh no, we're not. We spend ten minutes queueing for a No. 27 bus and we think we know it all. But believe me, compared with the Russians, we know nothing. They spent 70 years queueing for a loaf of bread and they know every trick in the book. Time and time again I'd blink, or bend down to talk to a child, and that would be it. A man-mountain would nip in front.

And I was loath to cough discreetly and tap him on the shoulder, since the shoulder in question was invariably enlivened with some sort of special forces tattoo. A baby being torn in half by two bulldozers. A dagger in a kneecap. That sort of thing.

Let's be honest, shall we. These guys were in Dubai. They were spending probably £1,000 a day on their hotel rooms. They had digital cameras that made the Japanese look backward and satphones that could steer the space station. And you don't get that sort of hardware, or holiday, by writing poetry. They were mafia, and that meant they were ex-KGB or Spetsnaz.

Only last year I heard of a Russian holidaymaker in the south of France. Like so many visitors to the Côte d'Azur, he was drawn to a villa on the coast and went to see an estate agent about it. '*Pardon, monsieur,*' said the estate agent. '*Mais il n'est pas possible de visiter cette maison parce qu'elle n'est pas à vendre.*'

This obviously displeased the Russian because the following morning the estate agent was found buried head down on the beach, with just his feet sticking out of the sand. And that's the thing about Russians. We wear a No Fear T-shirt. They wear the look in their eyes.

And that's why I chose not to laugh at their swimming trunks. However, I'm home now so I don't mind telling you they were hilarious. Like Speedos but without the style, and a bit tighter.

Still, they were better dressed than their wives. Elsewhere in the world the thong bathing suit is the preserve of Peter Stringfellow or size-eight girls. In Russia it is also worn by people who are eight tons or 80 years old.

Now I'm told that there are some extremely beautiful Russian girls. But obviously they're all on the internet, because the ones in Dubai were like turnips.

Except one, who was like nothing on earth. Let's start with her breasts, which were not vast. Vast is too small a word to convey the scale. When her boyfriend, who had a tattoo of two hammerhead sharks eating a man's eyes on his forearm, chose them from the catalogue, he'd probably been tempted by the ones marked 'massive'. But in the end he'd gone for the top of the range. The ones known in medical circles as: 'Oh, my God. They're moving towards us.'

The area underneath them had its own micro-climate. And yet they were not the first thing I noticed about the girl to whom they were attached.

The first thing I noticed were her lips, which were so full of collagen she looked like an orang-utan. An orang-utan with a pigtail.

And two full-scale models of the R101 in her bikini

top. I spent such a long time looking at her that when I looked back again, half of Ukraine had slipped in front of me in the queue.

Eventually I did get a ride, though, in a sort of big canal where giant waves came along every so often and made you go upside down. It was fun until I crashed into a woman who had obviously eaten so much pizza she'd begun to look like one.

Either that or she'd been to Chernobyl for her holidays. Each wave removed not so much a layer of skin as a lump of it.

There's something else about the Russkies, too. They made no effort to smile or chat. At least the Germans are happy to come over and apologise for their country's conduct in the war. The Russians still look like they're fighting it.

Sunday 12 January 2003

In Terror Terms, Rambo Has a Lot to Answer For

Do you remember the television show *Dallas*? If you do, you might recall a character called Cliff Barnes who was a bit of a loser, a bit of a joke.

He was in the oil business, like his father. He was born and raised in Texas. He became known on the international stage . . . Remind you of anyone?

Just a thought. Anyway, after the skyscraper business in New York, Cliff talked at some length about the long memory of the American warrior and how no stone would be left unturned in the search for the men responsible and in particular, Osama bin Laden.

Finding the men responsible was never going to be easy, since they were buried under a couple of million tons of rubble.

But it turns out that finding bin Laden was even harder.

They had a good look round Afghanistan and a cursory sweep of Pakistan but now, obviously, someone's lost the big atlas because they seem to have given up and decided to have a war with Iraq instead.

So does this mean that Ozzie is off the hook? No, not a bit of it, because he is now to be hunted down by the world's most fearless and monosyllabic soldier.

Yes, the CIA with its sophisticated spies in the sky

failed to find him. And even though they blew up every cave from Iran to Turkmenistan, the American air force failed to kill him. So now it's time to wheel out the human nuke.

Enter, with a fireball in the background and his locks flowing in the wind, Sylvester Stallone, who announced last week that Rambo, the 1980s superhero, is set to return.

And guess what? He's off to Afghanistan to stab some Taliban and mastermind a plot which brings bin Laden to justice.

This is likely to be tricky since the last time we saw Rambo, back in 1988, he was fighting with the mujahidin against the Russians in a film that was dedicated, and I quote, 'to the gallant people of Afghanistan'.

I actually took the trouble of watching *Rambo III* last week and, with the benefit of hindsight, it was hysterically prophetic. There's this marvellous scene when an American colonel is berating his Russian captors with these fine words: 'Every day your war machine loses ground to a bunch of poorly armed and poorly equipped freedom fighters.

'The fact is you underestimated your enemy. If you'd checked your history, you'd know that these people here have never given up to anyone. They'd rather die.'

Now we know that Hollywood is capable of some howlers. Who can forget *U571*, in which a brave American submarine crew captured an Enigma decoding device from the Nazis and won the war?

Then there was *Pearl Harbor*, in which a brave American pilot, flying a superior American fighter plane, won the battle of Britain and won the war again.

I know what you're going to say: that in films, dramatic licence is more important than rigid historical fact.

We leave the historical fact to our politicians, like Tony Blair, who famously told Cliff how the Americans had stood bravely at our side during the Blitz.

However, most people do not read newspapers. They change channels when the television news comes on. And they do not snuggle up at night with a nice Simon Schama. They get their history and current affairs from the cinema, and that's why the people who make films bear some responsibility for the course of world events.

I wonder, for instance, how much money Noraid might have raised if the IRA were not ceaselessly portrayed in Hollywood films as genial, whiskey-swilling freedom fighters with a real and noble grudge against the wicked colonial British.

Time and again we saw Richard Harris in a smart overcoat giving presents to children while marauding gangs of British squaddies drove their armoured Land Rovers over a selection of prams and pushchairs.

So when the boys came round your bar with the collecting tins, well, hey dude, have a dollar.

They no doubt did much the same after they saw *Rambo III* and now they probably feel like a bunch of chumps.

Who knows? Perhaps the young men of Algeria saw it, too, and thought: 'My, those Afghans look brave and fearless. We must join forces with them as soon as possible.'

I learnt the other day that one of the ancient enemies of the Afghans wrote a poem about them: 'May God deliver us from the venom of the cobra, the teeth of the tiger and the vengeance of the Afghan.'

Stallone would be well advised to remember that as he puts *Rambo IV* into production. Because if this film is as stupid and as irresponsible as its predecessor, it might just provoke some 'freedom fighter' to drive his 'holy war' into the side of the Sears Tower.

America is not invincible – but unfortunately Cliff probably doesn't understand this.

In the world he comes from, you die and then a few years later you come back to life in the shower.

Sunday 19 January 2003

House-Price Slump? It's the School Run, Stupid

So the value of your six-bedroom country house with its six-acre garden has fallen from £6 million to £600,000 in the past six days. *Country Life* magazine is chock-full of advertisements for properties that have been on the market for months. Huge discounts are there for the taking. And how do you double the value of a Gloucestershire house? Simple. Put in carpets and curtains.

According to the experts, this meltdown in the shires is because nobody's job is safe in EC1 and City bonuses are much smaller than usual. Really? Well, first let's find out who these 'experts' are.

When a former public schoolboy moves to London, his options are limited. The bright ones end up in banking, while those who are only one plum short of a fruit salad do stockbroking. Those who are mildly daft end up in insurance and those who are borderline idiotic wind up behind the counter in Hacketts.

That leaves Rupert. He needs a job where he can wear a suit or else he won't get invited to the right drinks parties in Fulham. But Rupert cannot add two and two without falling over. Rupert thinks Tim Nice-But-Dim is a documentary. So Rupert is an estate agent. That makes him an expert on house prices.

Now Rupert reckons that it's all falling apart in the

countryside because he met some chap at a 'do' last week who had just been fired from Goodyear, Stickleback and Bunsen Burner. 'Poor chap. Was going to buy a house in Hampshire. Now he can't afford it.'

Oh dear, Rupert, you are wide of the mark. Sure, City bonuses affect the market, but only slightly and only in Surrey. How many City boys are there in Alnwick or the Trough of Bowland? Scotland, too, is far beyond the reach of a commuter train – as is the West Country. How, pray, do City bonuses affect the price of a recent barn conversion in Milford Haven?

I live in what *Tatler* magazine once called the country's 'G-spot'. I am less than an hour from Notting Hill but by the same token I'm only five miles from Jilly Cooper Central in Gloucestershire. This is the Cotswolds and thanks to a local wildlife park there are more white rhinos up here than there are City boys.

So if it's not people in stripy shirts tightening their purse strings, what has brought the whole market to its knees?

Well, I know five families who live within three miles of where I am sitting now. Each has a substantial wisteria-softened eighteenth-century house with a pool, views that would make Elgar priapic and enough land to control their own sight lines. And all of them are moving out.

This has nothing to do with hunting. Since none of these people ride, none of them care. Nor does it have anything to do with foot-and-mouth. They may own land, but only so as to stop anyone doing anything with it.

Furthermore, it has nothing to do with the closure of the local bank or post office. These people have Range Rovers and staff to post their letters. So why, then, are they leaving in such vast numbers that suddenly the countryside has become a forest of 'for sale' signs?

It is the school run. Their children go to school in Oxford, which is eighteen miles away. During the day it is a 25-minute drive, which is not ideal but it's bearable.

However, in the morning it's an hour and a half and that is simply too much. The children need to be up at 6.30 a.m. and in the car by 7.15 a.m. They have to eat their breakfast out of Tupperware containers on the way. It's even worse at night because they don't get home until six. By the time they've done their prep, their music practice, had supper and a bath, it's bedtime. That is no life for a six-year-old.

So while the parents may be blissfully happy in their Cotswold stone palaces, they are moving into the centre of Oxford for the sake of their children's sanity.

To cure this, the local council, which is borderline insane when it comes to roads, will undoubtedly follow in the footsteps of London and impose a congestion charge, which will add £100 a month to the already significant school fees.

It will argue, of course, that the children should go on the bus, but they are six years old, for crying out loud – whatever Uncle Ken Livingstone says.

So then the local Nazis will argue that they shouldn't be going to school so far away. True, probably, but that is a decision people can make on their own. They don't need some woman with a bicycle knitted out of bits of her husband's beard to make the decision on their behalf.

What's to be done? The solution is simple. There are five families, each with two children, each doing the school run every morning. Why not club together to buy a minibus? The cost is minimal, it can go in the bus lane so the time saving is immense, you are happy, the eco-beards are happy and that just leaves Rupert.

Rupert is not happy because his friends in the City are still losing their jobs, but the country-house market has repaired itself overnight: 'Gosh. This analysis business is harder than I thought.'

Exactly. Stick to breathing. It's the only thing you're any good at.

Sunday 26 January 2003

The Lottery will Subsidise Everything, Except Fun

There's some doubt about whether the country can afford to back a bid for the Olympics in 2012. The money, we're told, would be better spent on the bottomless pits of health and education.

Oh, for crying out loud. We are the fourth-richest country in the world. If the Greeks can organise a fortnight of running and jumping, then for God's sake why can't we?

Sure, the £5 billion it would cost to host this big sports day would pay for an awful lot of baby incubators with plenty left over to house the refugees and fit new hips to every old lady in the country. But that's like spending all your surplus family income on insurance and piggy banks. Just occasionally you've got to say 'what the heck' and bugger off to Barbados for a fortnight.

What we need is some job demarcation here. We let the government look after the dull, worthy stuff and then we have a separate organisation solely concerned with making us feel good about living in this overcrowded, grey and chilly island. It won't be allowed to buy hips so nobody can complain when it doesn't.

The national lottery should have been that organisation, but sadly it's more dour and Presbyterian than Gordon Brown's drinks cabinet.

It has a remit to provide funding in six areas. First, there's 'the arts', which in principle is far too noble and which in reality means pumping money into small black-and-white films about an Asian woman who does nothing for a year.

Then there are charities, sports, projects to celebrate the millennium (they mucked that one up) and health, education and the environment. Why? Why use our fun money to pay for more bloody baby incubators – that's the government's job.

My real *bête noire*, however, is the final category. Nearly 5p in every lottery £1 (£300 million a year) goes on 'heritage'. If you don't know what that means, here are some of the organisations applying for grants.

The Royal Parks Agency wants £428,000 to conserve and restore Bushy Park, by Hampton Court. Nope, sorry, tell the Queen to pay for it.

Then we have the Museum of Advertising and Packaging, which wants £948,000 to pay for some new buildings. What? All the richest people in the country are in advertising and packaging. You want £948,000? Go and see the Rausings.

Here's a good one: Age Concern Northumberland would like £38,900 for a project called Meals on Wheels for Garden Birds. No, no, no, no, you can't have it – it's too dull.

The list of applicants runs into the thousands and while there's no list of who gets what in the end, you can use the search engine. I started by typing in 'multi' and 'cultural' and the poor computer nearly exploded. 'Church' had a similar effect.

Why is lottery money being used to restore churches? The church is richer than royalty. It's even richer, I'm told, than Jonathan Ross. If it needs a few bob to replaster a nave or two, it should think about bringing in bigger audiences. And if it can't put enough bums on seats, it should think about packing up. Or performing only in Germany. That's what Barclay James Harvest did.

But why is lottery money being used for 'heritage' in the first place? Maintaining the fabric of the country is surely the responsibility of the government. Lottery money should be spent on building new stuff designed only to make us feel good.

The government buys the baby incubators, which are 'useful'. The lottery buys us statues, which are 'amazing'.

Take Parliament Square in London. It's an island surrounded on all sides by three lanes of snarling diesel engines. You can't get to it and there's no point in going anyway unless you want to while away an afternoon looking at the guano on Winston Churchill's hat.

It is therefore the perfect place for lottery money to be spent on a huge new fountain.

In this country, most people's idea of a fountain is some cherub having a wee.

Last year the Fountain Society gave its award for best new water feature to Sheffield for its cascade in the Peace Gardens. It's good, especially at night, but (comparatively speaking) it's a bit of a Dimmock.

Think of Vienna where crystalline water gushes from every hole in every paving stone, or Paris where giant cannons fire trillions of gallons into a frenzy of rainbows under the Eiffel Tower.

In Dubai you have the seven-star Burj Al Arab. It's the best hotel in the world, more flunkies than an Edwardian tea party, rooms the size of Wales, food to stump A. A. Gill and views from the top-floor restaurant of F-15s lining up on their Baghdad bomb runs. It has everything.

But all anyone who has been there talks about is the fountain in the lobby.

Fountains can do that. Everyone loves a fountain and Parliament Square is the perfect place to build the mother of all water features.

The 'heritage' lottery fund could easily afford it – although the Museum of Advertising and Packaging might be disappointed – and there would still be enough left over for an observatory in the Peak District, a lattice-work bridge of ice and light over the M1, an Angel of the South and, with a bit of saving, a dirty great Olympic stadium in 2012.

Sunday 2 February 2003

The Shuttle's Useless, But Book Me on the Next Flight

Momentous news. George Bush has said something sensible. At a memorial service for the seven astronauts who died last Saturday he said: 'This cause of exploration and discovery is not an option we choose; it is a desire written in the human heart.'

Fine words. But this is America, a country where nobody is allowed to die of anything except extreme old age, and only then after a lengthy public inquiry. So instead of ploughing on with more journeys of 'exploration and discovery', the space shuttle has been grounded.

The message is clear. They're telling us that the crew's safety is paramount, but if that's the case why does the space shuttle have no ejection hatch? That may sound silly but back in 1960 the boffins didn't think so, because they sent a chap called Joe Kittinger to an altitude of 102,800 feet in a helium balloon. That's almost twenty miles up, by the way, and to all intents and purposes is space.

Once he reached the correct height he opened the door of his capsule . . . and jumped. Moments later he became the first man to break the sound barrier, without a plane, as he tore past 714 mph. The thickening air slowed him gradually until, at 17,000 feet, he opened his main parachute, landed gently in the New Mexico desert, had a cigarette and went home for tea.

A couple of years ago I met the guy – he now flies an aerial-signwriting biplane in California – and he was absolutely convinced that if the shuttle had had an escape hatch the crew of *Challenger* would be alive today.

But what of *Columbia*? NASA officials say they will leave 'no stone unturned' in their quest to find out what went wrong. It's hard to know precisely what this means. Bush said he would leave 'no stone unturned' in the hunt for Osama bin Laden. So on that basis NASA will probably look under a few rocks in eastern Texas and then declare war, for no obvious reason, on France.

Piecing *Columbia* together again and trying to figure out what went wrong is a PR stunt. Plainly, in a 20-year-old craft that's been to space 28 times there is no design fault. Whatever went wrong was an accident and even if they do work out what it was, it won't stop accidents happening. They could cure cancer but people would still die of heart attacks.

The law of averages now says that there will be a shuttle crash every ten years.

The law of probability says that if you launched one tomorrow it would be fine. But there won't be a launch tomorrow. And the way people are talking there might never be a launch again.

Some say there's no need for manned space flight any more. Others point at the space station and say it's a scientific red herring. And inevitably the *Guardian* asks how many baby incubators could be bought with the $15 billion (£9.1 billion) that it costs to keep NASA going every year.

This makes me so angry that my teeth itch. *Columbia* was named after Columbus, for crying out loud: what if he'd decided not to cross the Atlantic because it was a bit scary?

Then you have Chuck Yeager. In 1963 he was presented with a Starfighter NF 104. He knew that when the nose was angled up by 30 degrees then air no longer passed over the tail fin and that it would spin. He knew that the ejector seat fired downwards. He knew that it was called the Widowmaker by other pilots. But he still tried to fly one into space. That doesn't make him a hero. It makes him a human.

Yes, I know the shuttle's only real role these days is to service the space station and yes, I'm sure that seeing whether geraniums can flower in zero gravity will only slightly increase our insight into the workings of the universe. But we're missing the point. What the space station does is not important. What matters is the fact that we can build such a thing.

It's the same story with the shuttle itself. I've been to the factory in Louisiana where they refurbish the giant fuel tanks that are fished from the ocean after each mission. I've been to one of the rocket tests up the road in Stennis and it's like listening to the future.

I've even been allowed to sit in the cockpit of a shuttle and press buttons. Yes, it's ugly and yes, it's expensive. But never forget that this machine generates 37 million horsepower and is doing 120 mph by the time its tail clears the tower.

Remember, too, that the temperature on its nose as it re-enters the Earth's atmosphere is hotter than the surface of the sun.

The shuttle – one of the most intriguing and awesome technological marvels of the modern age – is America's only worthwhile gift to the world.

Would I put my money where my mouth is? Would I climb aboard if they launched one tomorrow? Absolutely, without a moment's hesitation.

And I would do so with some other unusually wise words from Bush ringing in my ears. 'Each of [the *Columbia* astronauts] knew great endeavours are inseparable from great risks and each of them accepted those risks willingly, even joyfully, in the cause of discovery.'

Sunday 9 February 2003

When the Chips are Down, I'm with the Fatherland

Following the rousing anti-war speech made by Germany's foreign minister last week, I would like to proclaim that from now on '*Ich bin ein Berliner*'.

Yes, I know this actually means 'I am a doughnut' but it gets my point across perfectly well. And my point is this . . .

When was the last time you heard one of our politicians talking so very obviously from the heart? Fuelled by passion rather than a need to keep on the right side of his party's PR machine, Joschka Fischer laid into Donald Rumsfeld, slicing through the American nonsense with a very simple and very effective 'I don't believe you'.

Over the years I have said some unkind things about the Krauts, but from now on, and until I change my mind, the teasing will stop. So sit back, slot a bit of Kraftwerk into your Grundig, light up a West, take a sip of your Beck's and let's have a canter through some of the Fatherland's achievements over the years.

We think *Trainspotting* was clever but let's not forget that back in 1981 two chaps from *Stern* magazine wrote an immeasurably more powerful drug movie called *Christiane F*. And while I'm at it, *Das Boot* was a much better submarine film than *Morning Departure*, in which Richard Attenborough's upper lip momentarily unstiffened for no discernible reason. In fact, *Das Boot* is probably the best film ever made.

What about comedy? It's often said that the Germans don't have a sense of humour, but look at it this way. They may laugh at desperately unfunny stuff such as *Benny Hill* and *Are You being Served?*, but who made it in the first place?

Then we have music. Quite apart from Haydn, Handel, Brahms, Beethoven and Bach, can you think of a better pop tune than Nena's '99 Red Balloons'? Bubblegum with a political undertone, and you never got that from Bucks Fizz.

Other things that the Germans gave the world include contact lenses, the globe, the printing press, X-rays, the telescope and Levi-Strauss; and chemistry lessons would have been a lot less fun were it not for the Bunsen burner.

What else? Well, it was Frank Whittle who invented the jet engine, there's no doubt about that, but the Luftwaffe had jets in its planes long before we did.

Similarly, the Americans and the Russians spent most of the 1960s fighting to gain supremacy over one another in space, but both were using German scientists and German rockets.

Got a Range Rover? That's German these days and so is the new Mini, the new Bentley, the new Rolls-Royce, the new Bugatti, the new Lamborghini and all new Chryslers. The Rover 75 is German, the entire Spanish car industry is German and by this time next year I bet they'll have Ferrari, Alfa Romeo, Lancia and Fiat as well.

Out in the Middle East, German soldiers may be a bit thin on the ground but the planes we're flying are largely German and let's not forget our SA80 rifles. They were designed and built in Britain but they didn't work, and all of them have had to be fixed by Heckler & Koch. Which is German.

I don't know very much about football but I do know that the result in 1966 and the 5–1 drubbing in Munich were freak occurrences. Normally their players make ours look disabled. And it's the same story in tennis, motor racing, gliding, invading Poland and skiing.

In fact, the only way we can beat the Germans at sport is by inventing games which they're too clever to play. Such as cricket, for instance, and that ice thing where women do the vacuuming in front of a kettle.

I should also like at this point to explain that I'd walk over Kate Winslet's head to get to Nastassja Kinski.

Of course, when it comes to food the Germans are rubbish. We're much better thanks to our top chefs like Marco Pierre White, Angus Steak House and Raymond Blanc.

Eurosceptics are forever asking who we want running the country: Tony Blair or a bunch of unelected German bankers. Well, since I'd rather have a weevil than His Tonyness, I'd have to go for the bankers.

Let's face it: if a German Tube train grazed a wall, lightly injuring a handful of people on board, they'd tow it away, replace the damaged track and have the network up and running by morning. Also, when their roads are coated with a thin veneer of snow, they send out a fleet of snow ploughs. The notion that you might be stuck on an autobahn for twenty hours because of inclement weather is utterly preposterous.

So what that they all like to belong to a club – there's a society in Cologne 'for the appreciation of the Irish postal service' – and so what if you aren't allowed to mow your lawn on a Sunday.

Given the big choice of being ordered about by Gerhard Schroder, or Rumsfeld, I wouldn't hesitate for a moment.

America likes to talk about how it saved Europe from tyranny twice in the past century. True, but let's not forget that they were unbelievably late on both occasions. Predictably, the Germans were as punctual as ever. I like that in a man. I like it in a nation, too. And that's why this week I am mostly a doughnut.

Sunday 16 February 2003

Save the Turtles: Put Adverts on Their Shells

It's been a bad week for the world's wildlife with the news that macaque monkeys have joined a list of 300 species in which the females are known to prefer girl on girl action to proper sex with a male.

It was also revealed that the formidable leatherback turtle has been put on the endangered list. But because the turtle spends most of its life half a mile below the surface of the sea, scientists have been unable to say whether the scarcity of numbers is due to rampant lesbianism or ruthless Mexican tuna fishermen.

Either way it's a shame because the leatherback has been around for 100 million years.

Indeed, some of the more aristocratic examples, such as the Leather Back Smythes for instance, can trace their family trees back to a time when the seas were patrolled by plesiosauruses. And that beats the hell out of the Fitzalan-Howards who go back only to 1066.

So what's to be done? Well, I've often argued that the best way to kick-start a dying species is to start eating it. No, really. If someone could convince the *Observer* housewives of Hoxton and Hackney in east London that the best way to put a sheen back in their hair was a daily bowl of giant panda chunks, someone, somewhere, would figure out a way to get the lazy sods breeding again.

However, I'm not sure this would work with a leatherback. I've eaten snakes, dogs, small whole birds in France and crocodiles, but Tommy Turtle is my line in the sand. I don't care if turtles turn out to be the antidote for cancer, I'm not eating even a small part of one and that's that.

Don't worry, though. I do have a suggestion which should help in these troubled times. I suggest that we use their shells as advertising hoardings.

Why not? In the olden days, advertisements were limited to books, television and town-centre hoardings, but now you find them everywhere.

Every time I log on to the internet, I'm asked if I would like a bigger penis (yes, but not if it comes with a virus), so why not advertise on the back of a turtle? It moves slowly up the beach and is watched intensely by lots of people who may well be interested in buying, say, a new pair of binoculars.

Think. The nozzle of the petrol pump urges you to buy a Snickers bar when you are in the Shell shop and, as you queue to board a plane, the airport tunnel is festooned with reasons for switching to HSBC. It seems that the decision on where to put your money has now come down to finding out which bank manager can make hand signals in Greece without causing offence.

Then, when you get off the plane, the luggage trolley advertises all the new and exciting ways of getting to the city centre. Even the back of a parking ticket is now a mini-hoarding.

In the days of George Dixon, phone boxes were boxes in which you found a phone.

But not any more. Now they are full of advertisements for young asylum ladies from Albania as well, curiously, as posters which talk about the advantages of having a mobile phone.

Have you been in a London taxi lately? The undersides of the foldaway seats carry advertisements telling you to put an advertisement there. I got a mailshot last week asking me to sponsor a child. Does that mean some poor African orphan has to walk around with 'Watch Jeremy Clarkson' on his forehead?

Advertisers have bought up every square inch of everywhere where people stand still. I went to a pub the other day which had adverts in front of the urinals and it's the same story in lifts, cinemas, Tube trains and, I presume, buses.

Fancy chilling out in some remote beauty spot where you can get away from the hurly-burly of consumerism? Forget it. Chances are you'll find a bench complete with a plaque advertising some dead person who also liked to sit there.

In town centres, every hanging basket and roundabout is sponsored, although on the open road things are better. Advertisers are banned from putting hoardings within sight of a motorway, but don't think you are safe. If Melvyn Bragg's arts programme on Radio 4 becomes too incomprehensible and you flick over to Classic FM, pretty soon you'll be brought down to earth and invited to buy your very own garden furniture.

The only problem is that the sheer number of people needed to find places for these adverts, and the even bigger number needed to sell the space, means that in the end there'll be nobody left to make anything worth advertising.

I went to Sheffield last week and was horrified to note that the vast steelworks have been pulled down to make way for an equally vast shopping centre which, presumably, can exist only because all the people who used to make knives and forks are now employed advertising the shopping centre.

Soon advertising agencies will be the only businesses left. That's bad for the economy but irrelevant as far as the turtle is concerned. He doesn't care whether it says Corus on his shell or Saatchi Cohen and Oven Glove. Just so long as it says something.

Sunday 23 February 2003

Give Me a Moment to Sell You Staffordshire

Boo. Hiss. Ref-er-ee. In last week's controversial *Country Life* poll to find Britain's nicest and nastiest counties, Staffordshire was named the worst place in all England.

At first I assumed that being a *Country Life* survey it would have nothing to do with the real world. I thought they would have counted the number of monogrammed swimming pools in each county, divided that by the availability of arugula and added the number of hunts to come up with Devon as a winner.

But no. They've been quite thorough, looking at house prices, the weather, the efficiency of the local council, the quality of the pubs, tranquillity, the arts, the lot. And they ended up with a list that had Devon, Gloucestershire and Cornwall at the top (Cornwall? Have they never seen *Straw Dogs*?) and Staffordshire at the bottom.

Now I admit that Staffordshire is a bit like one of those lost cities in Egypt. We know it to be there. We can see it on maps. And it's written about in books. But nobody knows where it is exactly.

Plus, it's ringed by places of such horror that even Indiana Jones would think twice about trying to go there. He may have faced runaway balls and poisoned darts in his quest for the lost ark but should he, one day, mount an expedition to locate the ancient city of Stafford, he will have to go through either Wales, Birmingham or Cheshire. Grisly.

I know where Staffordshire is because I spent most of my most interesting years there. I went to school about half a mile from it, my virginity went west in Yoxall, I got my first speeding ticket on the A38 outside Barton-under-Needwood, and it was in Abbots Bromley that I learnt how to be chemically inconvenienced, how to be thrown out of a pub, how to be chucked by a girlfriend without blubbing, how to drive fast, how to do everything that matters, really.

No, honestly. In the Coach and Horses I learnt that it was possible to snog a girl and play pool at the same time. You don't pick up a trick like this in Tiverton, that's for sure.

I remember, too, going home from parties in those misty dawn mornings that were a hallmark of that baking summer of 1976. Across the Blithfield Reservoir on the boot of some girl's mother's Triumph Stag, Bob Seger's *Night Moves* on the eight-track. That was Staffordshire and God it was good.

So when I saw the result of the *Country Life* survey I was horrified.

Staffordshire worse than Hertfordshire? Worse than Essex? Worse than East Sussex and even Surrey? Rubbish. If Kent is the garden of England, then Surrey is its patio.

Staffordshire, however, is one of its lungs. The rolling

farmland near Uttoxeter, replete with wisteria villages, is as delightfully English as anywhere in the country and the Cannock Chase on a damp autumn morning, with the dew in the ferns, is like Yosemite, without the cliffs to fall off or the bears to eat you.

Actually, to be honest, it's not like Yosemite at all, but there is a lot of wildlife. Deer. Deer. More deer. If you're really lucky, you might catch a glimpse of a great crested Lord Lichfield stomping about the woods. And where does the Duke of Devonshire live? Derbyshire, that's where.

Mind you, he's about the only thing that has come out of Devon. I'm struggling now to think of anything in my house that was made there. And you could spray the county with machine-gun fire without hitting a single musician, artist or rock band. You wouldn't hit a pheasant either. The bloody things are all far too high.

Whereas Staffordshire is the birthplace of your lavatory bowl, the Climax Blues Band, Dr Johnson, all your crockery and Robbie Williams. It's also home to my oldest friend, who has the best name in the history of speech: Dick Haszard. And even better, his uncle's a major.

I was explaining all of this to the man who edits my column. There was lots of puffed-up indignation and tutting. So we agreed that I wouldn't write, as planned, about that Swiss yacht winning the America's Cup and that I would write in defence of Staffordshire.

Sadly, though, I can't. The problem is the towns. Stafford. Lichfield. Stoke.

They're all ghastly. And it's all very well having the Cannock Chase, but it's named after Cannock, which would be the worst town in the world were it not for Burton upon Trent. Rugeley is a power station. Tamworth is a pig, Newcastle under Lyme is just confusing and Uttoxeter is hard to spell. All you can buy on the high street in any of these places is a house or a hamburger, and at night all any of them offer is a polyurethane tray of monosodium glutamate and the promise of coming home with a beer bottle sticking out of your left eye.

I still maintain that it's not the worst county. I'd far rather live in Staffordshire than Surrey but, and this is a serious point, trying to argue that you'd have a good time there because I did 25 years ago is daft. Nearly as daft, in fact, as those professional Scousers who from their piles on the banks of the Thames still maintain that Liverpool's the greatest place on Earth. Well, if that's the case, Cilla, why don't you push off back to Walton?

Sunday 9 March 2003

A Quick Snoop Behind the Queen's Net Curtains

Last week the Queen of England very kindly agreed to break off from her waving duties and lend a hand with a television programme I'm making about the Victoria Cross.

And so on Wednesday I slipped into a whistle and went to Buckingham Palace to see some prototype medals she'd found in a cupboard. Sadly, I never met my new researcher but I did have a snout around the state rooms, which provided a rare insight into the life of the royals.

First of all, I've never really understood why the richest and most powerful of the world's royal families has to live behind a *Coronation Street*, working-class veil of net curtains. There are no nets at Versailles, for instance. But it turns out they are weighted at the bottom and designed to catch flying glass should someone set off a bomb.

That's something you and I don't have to worry about, and nor do we have to share our house with 500 staff, most of whom, it seems, will one day take the tabloid shilling and spill the beans on your toiletry habits.

Then there's the bothersome business of guests. Last week the new president of Albania was scheduled to make a twenty-minute visit. Imagine what that must be like.

Going to meet him off the Eurostar and trying not to look surprised when he emerges, not from the carriage, but from a hidey-hole underneath the bogies.

Then she's got the weekly visits from His Tonyness. They probably weren't so bad when he was a new boy but now it must be awfully wearing to have to call him sir and kiss his shoes all the time.

Mind you, he's nothing compared with the ordinary people. Pretty well every day a bunch of hand-wringing do-gooders goes to the palace for an official function of some kind, and every single one of them, no matter how worthy they are, will feel an almost uncontrollable urge to nick something.

I did. Over the years I have been to hundreds of houses and have never once felt the need to pocket a teaspoon or an inkwell. But over a cup of tea in the palace's music room, I was overcome with a Herculean bout of kleptomania. I had my eye on the harpsichord but anything would have done. A cup. A saucer. A milk jug, even.

Staff, I'm told, keep a watchful eye on visitors but what do you say when you see a leading Rotarian shove a royal teapot in his pocket? How on earth do you ask for it back, diplomatically? I mean, he's going to know that you know that it didn't get in his trousers by accident.

And what's more, when Denise Van Outen boasted that she'd nicked an ashtray while on a trip to the palace

Mrs Queen couldn't very well prosecute. It would seem mean, somehow. The same goes for the old biddies who pick flowers while at the garden parties. Even Prince Philip has never been heard to yell: 'Oy, Ethel! Leave that orchid alone.'

Gravel, apparently, is what most people steal. Handfuls of it. Although my biggest problem with the loose shale that covers the courtyard was resisting the urge to do a handbrake turn on it.

The worst thing, though, about living in the palace is the decor. The Queen is the only person alive who watched that Michael Jackson shopping trip to Las Vegas and thought: 'I've got one of those vases.'

The whole thing is a symphony of gloomy portraits of unsmiling ancestors with splashes of pure ostentation and gilt. In the main corridor pink and gold Eltonesque sofas clash violently with the bright red carpets.

It's a Neverland kind of Derry Irvine hell and, unlike anyone else, the Queen can't watch an episode of *Homefront* and think: 'Right. I'll knock through here, fit a natural wood floor, some Moroccan-style scatter cushions and top it all off with a bit of rag-rolling on the ceiling.' She's stuck with it.

She's stuck with her job, too, endlessly waving and asking people to hand over the teapot. Of course, theoretically, she still has the power to start a war, though His Tonyness is capable of doing that on his own these days, and she can still dissolve Parliament.

This brings me on to my biggest point. Imagine having the power to send that braying bunch of ne'er-do-wells from the Palace of Westminster home, and not doing it.

Not even for a bit of fun, during a party. Whatever you may think of the Queen she has willpower, that's for sure.

You may argue that the pain of being a queen is eased by her vast fortune. This may be true. But what can the poor dear spend it on? A speedboat? A Lamborghini? She's not Victoria Beckham, you know.

Some say she should be replaced with a president. But who, at a cost to the nation of just 82p per person per year, is going to live in what amounts to Liberace's wardrobe, and spend their days making small talk with stuttering and sweaty two-bit Third World politicians whose entourage is hell-bent on nicking the carpet?

You'd need to be mad to volunteer for all this. But then presidents usually are.

Sunday 16 March 2003

Who Needs Abroad When You Can Holiday in Hythe?

What a week. With the blossom in the trees and the sun on our backs, the nation kicked off its shoes, sat back and split its sides at photographs of those holidaymakers in Italy, all cold and shivering under their umbrellas.

There was, however, a fly in the blueness of it all. Normally when the sun puts his hat on someone on the weather forecast will tell us precisely how long we can spend outside without catching cancer.

This week, however, the Ministry of Misery came up with a new idea. On Wednesday it announced that the warm weather may cause smog in the south-east and that this may lead to breathing difficulties.

Oh, for God's sake. What kind of sad, friendless person peels back his curtains on the sort of days we had last week and thinks: 'Oh no'? Well matey, whoever you are, just because you spend all weekend in the darkest corner of your mother's attic, downloading photographs of naked ladies, doesn't mean we have to as well. So get back to your internet and leave us alone.

This kind of thing doesn't happen in Italy or France. And even in the land of the healthy and the home of the safe you aren't warned on the radio to stay indoors whenever it stops raining. What you get there is: 'It's a beautiful morning in the Bay Area. We're expecting highs in the upper twennies. Here's the J Geils Band.'

What we get is: 'It's a beautiful morning in the south-east. We're expecting thousands of people to choke to death. Stay indoors. Stay white. Here's some Morrissey.'

However, despite the best endeavours of the killjoys, the pleasant weather did set me thinking. Was it right to laugh at the 1.8 million people who've gone away for Easter? Can you really have a good holiday here at home?

Those of you who spent Good Thursday in a jam are probably thinking: 'No, you cannot.' But actually, spending two hours in traffic listening to the radio is better than spending two hours checking in at an airport. In a jam nobody wants to look in your shoes, for instance.

There are some drawbacks, though. Wherever you go in Britain some clown on a two-stroke microlight will spend the day 100 feet above your head, battling pointlessly and noisily against a four-knot headwind.

But let's not forget that the Lonely Planet guide voted Britain the most beautiful island on earth.

There's variety, too. Readers of the *Sun* can go to Blackpool or Scarborough. The reader of the *Independent* can go to Wales, the readers of *Taxi* magazine can go to Margate. Readers of the *Observer*, all of them actually, can take their Saabs to one of those wooden fishing cottages on Dungeness, where they can spend a week pretending to be Derek Jarman and having angst about the nuclear power station.

And readers of the *Daily Mail*? Well, they can go to their cellars to avoid falling house prices, murderers and whatever plague it is that's going to kill them this week.

So what about you, readers of the *Sunday Times*? Well, obviously, you have Norfolk and Rock to play with, but if you fancy something different – very different – may I suggest the Imperial Hotel in Hythe?

As is usual in British south-coast provincial hotels, the heating was turned up far too high, the carpets were far too patterned and the chef had ideas far above his station. The menu was full of things nestling on other things.

But don't be fooled. Don't think this was just another British hotel that threw in the towel when cheap package holidays started in the 1960s. No, this place presented me with one of the most bewitching nights of my entire travelling life.

The dining room, for instance, featured an altar – and, on the far wall, some curtains, behind which, I can only presume, there was an oven. So when the older guests, so prevalent here on the south coast, drop dead in the soup, they can be cremated on site. 'You check in. We check you out.' Maybe that's the Imperial's motto.

I must also mention our waitress. She was a pretty little thing who laughed, and I mean like a drain, whenever anyone spoke to her.

After dinner she took me into a broom cupboard – I felt a Boris Becker moment coming on but sadly it was not to be. She needed to explain, she said, that she was joyful because she has Jesus Christ Our Saviour inside her. Lucky old Jesus.

The bar was full of dead pensioners, a group who said they were 'tri-service people' but were actually 00 agents, and all the German baddies from *Die Hard*, who'd arrived on the lawn in a helicopter.

I therefore went to the lounge and guess what I found? If it had been a Roman orgy or a Ku Klux Klan meeting, I wouldn't have been surprised, but in fact there were 50 soldiers from the Chinese army in there. You don't find that sort of thing in Siena.

So will I be taking my summer holiday at the Imperial? No, not really. The Lonely Planet is right to say Britain is the most beautiful island on earth. But only as a place to live.

The most beautiful island to take a holiday on is Corsica.

Sunday 20 April 2003

We Have the Galleries, But Where's the Art?

The opening of Charles Saatchi's new gallery in London seems to have highlighted a problem. There are now so many galleries dotted around Britain that there simply isn't enough art to go round.

We saw this first with Bilbao's Guggenheim Museum, which sits like a big golden hat on the unkempt head of this otherwise unremarkable industrial city in northern Spain. It's an astonishing building, which is a good thing because the exhibits inside aren't astonishing at all.

When I went a couple of years ago there was a triangle, a very small maze and a frock. Further research has revealed that the most popular exhibition ever staged there was for customised motorcycles.

Now the disease has spread. All over Britain the dark satanic mills, which fell into disrepair when the empire crumbled, are being turned into art galleries. That may sound like a good idea at a meeting. But exactly how much art is there in Gateshead? Or Walsall?

Oh sure, rural pubs often encourage us to patronise 'local artists'. So we pat them on the head, call their work 'amazing', ask where they got the idea to paint with their eyes closed and then run for our lives.

The fact is that most of Britain's art is hung in the vaults of Japanese banks.

The rest is at the Tate or the National. So while it's jolly noble to turn a former duster factory in Glossop into a gleaming blend of low-voltage lighting and holly flooring, there is going to be a problem finding stuff to put on the walls.

The curators could turn to New York artist Maurizio Cattelan, whose recent works include a life-size sculpture of the Pope flattened by a meteorite that has supposedly crashed through the roof of the gallery. Then there's his replica of the Vietnam war memorial in Washington, DC, inscribed not with the names of dead soldiers but with every defeat suffered by the England football team.

There is, however, a problem with Cattelan's work. Next month, someone is expected to pay more than £200,000 for his 8-foot rabbit suspended by its ears. Were the buyer to be Walsall Borough Council, it's fair to expect some kind of voter backlash.

As I keep saying, everything these days is measured in terms of how many baby incubators or teachers it could have bought. As a result, if a council spends £200,000 on a dangling bunny it's going to find itself in the news-papers, that's for sure.

Even Saatchi struggles. Obviously unable to secure a nice painting of some bluebells by a local artist, he has filled his new gallery with all sorts of stuff that to the untrained eye is food, bedding, waste and pornography.

At the opening party he got 200 people to lie naked outside the doors and such was the unusualness of it all that Helen Baxendale, the actress, said she was nervous about talking to Tracey Emin 'in case she wees on me or something'.

Inside guests could feast their eyes on a pickled shark, a room half-filled with sump oil and a severed cow's head full of maggots and flies.

The high-profile nature of all this provides some hope for the owners of provincial galleries – they need only trawl their local butchers and fishmongers to fill half the space – but it's not so good for you and me.

The trouble is that thanks to Saatchi – and, to a certain extent, Laurence Llewelyn-Bowen – there's a sense that you can put anything on your walls at home and it will do. But it won't.

I, for instance, have a very nice little picture in my sitting room. It's of some cows on a misty morning by a river. I know this because it was painted by someone whose deftness with a brush meant he could represent cows and mist and a river.

Unfortunately, it gives off a sense that I'm not moving with the times. So really I should take it down and nail one of my dogs to the wall instead. Or maybe I should frame the Sunday joint and put that up.

It's hard to know what to do. I could go for a picture of Myra Hindley that was painted using the dingleberries from a sheep. But it would almost certainly cost £150,000.

With my flat in London I went for a look that's clean and clinical and minimalistic. Bare wooden floors and bare walls painted in one of those new colours that's nearly Barbie pink but not quite. If you were to photograph it and put it in a design magazine, it would look fantastic and people would pay £5 to come and look round.

But every time I walk through the door I always think: 'God, this place could do with some furniture.' The people living below probably think it could do with some carpets, too.

There's another problem. It's all very well subscribing to the 'design' phase we are going through at the moment, but soon there will be another phase and then you'll have to throw away your hardwood floors and start again.

It isn't so bad when your trousers become dated because it's only £50 for a new pair. But when you need a whole new house, that's a different story. Which is why my misty cows are staying. Real art, like real jeans, never goes out of fashion. You'll never hear anyone say: 'That Mona Lisa, she's so last week.'

Sunday 27 April 2003

You Think SARS is Bad? There's Worse Out There

As viruses go, SARS is pretty pathetic. It's hard to catch and not very powerful.

Despite the horror stories, 90 per cent of those who become infected go on to make a full recovery. On balance, then, it's probably sensible for schools in Britain to stay open and for aeroplanes to carry on circling the globe.

However, what if it were Ebola? Since this filovirus was first identified in 1976 it has become a bit of a joke. Reports at the time said it dissolved fat and lots of Hurley/Posh surgically enhanced women thought it might be a fun alternative to liposuction. I'm just as bad. Every time I go to the doctor I always tell him I've caught Ebola just for a laugh.

Actually, it isn't very funny. It attacks your immune system – but unlike HIV, which lets something else come along and kill you, Ebola keeps on going, charging through your body with the coldness of a shark and the ruthlessness of a Terminator.

First your blood begins to clot, clogging up your liver, kidney, lungs, brain, the lot. Then it goes for the collagen – the glue that holds your body together – so that your skin starts to fall off. Usually your tongue falls out, your eyes fill with blood and your internal organs liquefy before oozing out of your nose. Except for your stomach. You vomit that out of your mouth.

It's not an exaggeration to say that Ebola eats you alive and then, to make sure you don't die in vain, it finishes you off with a huge epileptic fit, splashing eight pints of massively infectious blood all over anyone within 20 feet or so.

Nobody dies of Ebola with dignity and very few victims get better. Unlike SARS, the most virulent strain of Ebola, called Zaire, kills 90 per cent of those who get it.

Now at this point you are probably thinking: so what? There is no Ebola in the world at the moment. Oh yes there is, but despite a twenty-year, multi-million-dollar hunt nobody has been able to find where it lives. Some say the host is a bat, others say it's a spider or a space alien. All we know is that occasionally, and for no obvious reason, someone comes out of the jungle with bleeding eyes and his stomach in a bag.

Tests have shown that the virus is simple and ancient. It has probably been hanging around since the days when Rio de Janeiro was joined at the hip to Cameroon. Over the years, therefore, it's reasonable to assume that it has killed thousands of people. But because it kills so fast it could never travel. Now, though, with Zaire connected to the worldwide web of airline routes, an infected person could reach London or New York before he knew he was ill.

We saw this with Aids. Who knows how long this had been hanging around in the jungle, playing jiggy-

jiggy with monkeys? When they paved the Kinshasa Highway that bisects Africa from east to west and the trucks started to flow, Aids burst into the world and, 25 years later, about 22 million people were dead.

It may be that in years to come, when Aids has killed more people than the First and Second World Wars combined, historians will look upon the building of this road as the most significant event of the twentieth century.

HIV, remember, is another pathetic virus. It can live for only twenty seconds in the air, it travels from person to person only if they engage in vigorous sex, and it takes ten years to do to a person what Ebola manages to do in ten days.

SARS has shown us just how devastating the jet engine can be as a carrier. A doctor gets poorly in a Hong Kong hotel and within weeks there are outbreaks all over the world. Even Canada got itself on the news.

Like HIV, SARS is also difficult to catch. Ebola is easy. In the 1990s scientists in America put an infected monkey in a cage on one side of a room and a healthy monkey in a cage on the other. Two weeks later the healthy monkey was dead.

Following a spate of Hollywood films, most people believe the human race is at greatest risk of annihilation from a giant meteorite or some kind of religious nuclear war. But if Ebola ever gets on a plane, experts say that 90 per cent of us will be dead within six months. It is known in America, where they are good at names, as a 'slate wiper'.

This is why I'm slightly nervous about the world's reaction to SARS. We like to think that governments have contingency plans for every conceivable disaster. But I got the impression over recent weeks that a lot of people have been sitting around in rooms saying 'ooh' and 'crikey' and 'you can't do that – think of the shareholders'.

What we need is a scheme that would allow scientists and medical experts to impose, at a moment's notice, a total ban on all flights and a global curfew. But who would run such a thing? The World Health Organisation doesn't even have big enough teeth to take a bite out of that political colossus Canada.

The Americans? I fear not. Any disease that has a fondness for eating stomachs would head there first. Besides, if they can't find Saddam and Osama, what chance do they have of finding something so small that there could be a million on the full stop at the end of this sentence.

So it's the United Nations then. We've had it.

Sunday 4 May 2003

Mandela Just Doesn't Deserve His Pedestal

It seemed like a foregone conclusion. A panel of arty types was asked by a local council whether a statue of Nelson Mandela should be erected in Trafalgar Square, right under the portals of the South African embassy.

Astonishingly, however, this week they said that no, it shouldn't. Now a selection of Labour MPs and Ken Livingstone have written to the *Guardian* to express their dismay.

I'm rather pleased. If we're going to have a Nelson theme in Trafalgar Square, I would rather see a bronze of Elvis wannabe Ricky Nelson, or the old tax dodger himself, Willie Nelson. Actually, come to think of it, what I'd really like is a stone immortalisation of the Nelson's Nelson, the Brazilian racing driver Nelson Piquet.

As you can see, my objections are not based on jingoistic principles. There are 30,000 statues in London and numbered among these are Gandhi in Tavistock Square and Abraham Lincoln in Parliament Square. I seem to remember there's a bronze of Oscar Wilde kicking around somewhere, too.

Also, I have no problem with any attempt to erect some powerful symbol about racial harmony slap bang in the middle of what was once the centre of the empire.

But if this is the goal, then I think we might be better off with a statue of Paul McCartney and Stevie Wonder. It could even be a musical statue serenading passers-by with the duo's 1982 hit, 'Ebony and Ivory'.

I have to be honest. I have a problem with Mandela. I know that he has become a symbol of democracy's triumph over evil and a hero to oppressed people everywhere, and I'm sure that Livingstone and Co. are right to say that millions of people would like to see this 'great statesman' immortalised for all time in the middle of London.

But he's not Gandhi, you know. You may like what he represents – I do – but if you peer under the halo of political correctness that bathes him in a golden glow of goodness you'll find that the man himself is a bit dodgy.

Back in the early 1960s he was the one who pushed the ANC into armed conflict. He was known back then as the Black Pimpernel. And his second marriage was to Winnie, who's now a convicted fraudster and thief with, we're told, a penchant for Pirelli necklaces.

Furthermore, since his release from prison and his eventual rise to the presidency Mandela has had some extraordinary things to say about world affairs.

He's deeply concerned, for instance, about the plight of one of the Lockerbie bombers and has expressed support for both Gadaffi and Castro.

Indeed, he has singled out Cuba, praising it for its human rights and liberty. I'm sorry – what human rights, what liberty? Perhaps he should go to the Cohiba nightclub and ask one of the twelve-year-old prostitutes which way her parents voted.

Once, while defending his decision to share a stage with three Puerto Rican terrorists who shot and wounded five US congressmen in 1954, Mandela said he supported anyone who was fighting for self-determination. The IRA, the Chechens, Shining Path? What if I started a movement to bring about independence for Chipping Norton; what if I blew up council offices in Oxford and shot a few policemen – could I count on Mandela's support?

What of the people who hijacked those airliners on 11 September? They would almost certainly have argued that one of their goals was self-rule for Palestine. So does he think their actions were justified? Confusingly, he doesn't.

I simply don't understand why the Nobel academy gave him a peace prize or why Charlie Dimmock and Alan Titchmarsh gave him a new garden. And I don't see why he should be given a statue in Trafalgar Square, either. If we're after someone who stands up for the oppressed, what about Jesus? I feel fairly sure that he never blew up a train.

However, what I would like to see is something to commemorate Frank Whittle. Here we have a man whose invention – the jet engine – turned the world into a village. And by bringing us closer together, who knows how many conflicts he has helped us to avoid?

More than that, who knows what might have happened in the Second World War, if only the air ministry had listened? For year after year the ministry ignored Whittle's invention, even refusing to pay a £5 fee to renew his patent in the 1930s.

Of course, in the latter stages of the war, when it saw jet planes shooting down V-2 rockets, it staged a serious about-face. Whittle was knighted, given a CBE, a KBE and £100,000. He was also promoted to air commodore. But he knew that Britain could have had jets before the war broke out and that, as a result, millions of lives could have been saved. In disgust he went to live in America, where he died just seven years ago.

Coventry remembers its most famous son by having a statue in the town of Lady Godiva. I'm told that Whittle has a bust in the RAF Club in Piccadilly but that's not good enough. He should be in Trafalgar Square. And it won't cost that much, either, since he was only 5 feet tall.

Sunday 11 May 2003

In Search of Lost Time, One Chin and a Life

When I was a child time used to pass with the languid sultriness of a saxophone solo. Every day the sun would amble through the cloudless sky as though it were being propelled by the gentlest of summer breezes. And then, in the winter, perfect crisp snow would settle and not melt for what felt like 40 years.

At school I remember spending those long, warm evenings listening to those long, warm songs on *Dark Side of the Moon*.

One of the tracks seemed to suggest that time passed quickly and that unless I got out of my chair, took off my Akai headphones and did something with my life, ten years would flash past and I'd still be 'kicking around on a piece of ground in my home town, waiting for someone or something to show me the way-e-yay'.

What a lot of nonsense, I thought. We received no drug education back then but we didn't need it. Pink Floyd were a living, breathing example of what recreational pharmaceuticals did to the mind. Ten years, as any teenage boy knows, is a century.

Pretty soon, I was 23 and time was still 'flexing like a whore', floating round and round as though it were a seed pod caught in the gurgling eddy of a mountain beck. If anything, there was even more time in my twenties than there had been in my childhood, largely because I wasted so little of it by sleeping.

However, when you get to 33, everything changes. Time straps a jet pack to its back, lights the afterburners and sets off at Mach 3. The sun moves across the sky as though God's got his finger on the fast forward button. Blink and you can miss a whole month.

This was hammered home on Thursday night, when I met up with a dozen friends for a pizza at a favourite old haunt of ours in Wandsworth. We used to go there a lot, in the early nineties, which, we all agreed, seemed like only yesterday.

That's weird, isn't it? No one ever says when they're twenty: 'Gosh. It only seems like yesterday that I was ten.' But my God, the time from when your dreams are smashed and you realise you'll never be a fighter pilot to the moment when your body starts to swell up and fall to pieces really does go by with the vim and vigour of a Kylie song.

When I was 20 my friends and I went to the pub. When I was 30 we still went to the pub. Nothing ever happened. Nothing ever changed. But then, all hell broke loose.

One of us moved to France, one died, one divorced, one has taken up golf, one (me) has grown six new chins, one has had a lung and most of his bottom removed, one is in a never-ending custody battle with his ex-wife, who seems to have been taken by the breeze of insanity, and two were moved from their penthouse flat by social services to secure accommodation in Uxbridge . . . for absolutely no reason at all.

Ten years ago we used to leave that restaurant whenever we ran out of money or, more usually, when the cellar ran out of wine. On Thursday we all left at eleven because we were tired.

I woke up at eight the following morning to find I had three more chins and a terrible hangover. And by the time that had gone another 30 years had whizzed by.

I cannot believe how fast time goes now. I leave the *Top Gear* studio, write this, say hello to the children and then I'm back in the studio again. It's like God has taken the job of marking time from Oscar Peterson and given it to the mad drummer Cozy Powell.

It's amazing. On Saturday afternoons we used to play Risk, simply to pass the time until the pub opened again. I had the space in my life to read books and not only listen to Pink Floyd songs but work out what they meant. I drove fast, only for fun. Now I drive fast to keep up with the clock.

I read with despair about people who give up London thinking that when they're far from the Tube and the expectant wink of a computer's cursor they can float through the days like dandelion seeds. It doesn't work because 'where you are' isn't the problem. It's 'when you are'.

In the olden days you got married in your teens, had children in your twenties, made a few quid in your thirties, enjoyed it in your forties and fifties and then retired in your sixties.

Now, you do nothing in your teens, nothing in your twenties and by the time you're 40 you're on the employment scrapheap, a seven-chinned hasbeen with a spent mind and man-breasts. This means you have to cram your whole life into your thirties.

And that's why it passes at 2,000 mph.

Well, I'm 43 now and I want the saxophone back. I want to lie on my back, chewing grass, thinking of nothing but what my final words might be.

My dad did that and came up with: 'Son, you've made me proud.' Adam Faith kept on charging and ended up with: 'Channel 5 is all s★★★, isn't it.'

An apology. Last week I said that jets were shooting down V-2 rockets at the end of the Second World War. Many people wrote to say it was V-1s. I should have checked, but I didn't have time. Sorry.

Sunday 18 May 2003

In Search of a Real Garden at the Chelsea Show

Every week I strap myself into a monstrously powerful car and hurtle round a test track in a blaze of tyre smoke and noise. It's a constant battle with the laws of physics, and that's a dangerous game to play. One day, inevitably, it'll end in tears.

Still, in a good week the television programme that results attracts 3.7 million viewers, making it the second-most watched show on BBC2.

Interestingly, and rather annoyingly, we're beaten by *Gardeners' World*, in which a man called Monty Don moves soil from one place to another and gets all excited about his new compost heap. What's more, so far as I can tell, he speaks mostly in Latin.

We see a similar sort of thing with live events. While the vibrant London Motor Show, with its bikini-clad lovelies, coughed up blood for a few years and then died completely, the Chelsea Flower Show continues to be a huge attraction. This year, it even managed to attract me.

I needed a fountain and perhaps a statue for a bit of garden that I've just paved.

I like paving. It doesn't need mowing and unlike grass, which is vindictive, it doesn't give me hay fever on purpose.

Unfortunately, at Chelsea this year, the most impressive water feature on display was the sky, so everyone was forced into a tent full of flowers. Flowers bore me.

They do nothing for 50 weeks of the year and then on the other two they continue to do nothing because you planted them somewhere that was too hot, too shady, too high up or too near sea level. And the soil was wrong too. And the wind.

Happily, the people weren't boring at all. At a motor show you queue with men called Ron and Derek for a pint of brown in a plastic glass. At Chelsea they give you champagne every time you stop moving and you get to see Cherie Blair in real life.

I was also interested to note that the whole event was quite smart. It's all sponsored by bankers on the basis, I suppose, that if people are interested in shrubs at £3,000 a pop, they might have a bit of floating lolly that needs licking into shape.

However, because it's smart, everyone was in a suit, which meant it was hard to spot the bankers coming. Is it Rowan Atkinson? Is it Prince Andrew? Oh bloody hell, it's a bloke from Merrill Lynch with news of his Swiss supersava scheme.

I escaped by seeking out the garden that had been done by people in prison. I don't get this. We're forever being told that prisoners are only allowed out of their cells for a moment's man-love in the showers, yet every year at Chelsea one nick or another turns up with a full-scale model of Babylon.

How, when they're not allowed outside? And where

do they get the soil? No really, if I were one of the guards, I'd have a look under the stove because I bet they'd find Charles Bronson down there in 'Harry', the *Great Escape* tunnel.

Eventually it stopped raining and I went outside to look at the statues. Why are they all of Venus? How come every single sculptor sits down with a block of stone and thinks: 'I know. I'll do that bird with no arms.' Why can't someone make a statue of Stalin? Or Keith Moon?

And if they do an animal, it's always an otter. Come on. You're artists. Use your imagination. If it has to be an otter, make it *Ring of Bright Water*'s Mij, with a shovel in the back of its head. In fact, why not make a statue of Hitler beating an otter to death. That's something I'd buy.

Then I got to the fountains. Oh deary me. Some of them were very clever. The silver and purple waves with a gentle cascade tippling down their flanks were marvellous and will undoubtedly look good when they end up where they belong: in the foyer of a businessmen's hotel at Frankfurt airport.

The thing is, I like a fountain to roar, not tinkle. What I want in my back garden is the Niagara on Viagra, and despite extensive searching, Chelsea couldn't help.

In fact, I saw nothing there that had any relevance at all. I stopped for a moment to admire one flower bed that was filled with crushed blue glass. It looked wonderful, a cheerful alternative to the dreary brownness of soil or bark.

I was just about to plunge my hand into the blueness for a feel when a man leapt out of nowhere. 'I wouldn't do that,' he warned, showing me his hands, which looked like they'd been through a bacon slicer. So what possible use is glass, then, as a substitute for mud? Unless you want to chop your dog's legs off?

I went home that night a bit dejected. And my mood darkened when I reached the house. Two years ago I planted a mixed hedge to separate my paddock from the road. It was just getting going, the little whips had become mini toddler trees.

But some berk in an untaxed, uninsured Sierra had lost control on the corner and smashed the whole thing to pieces. Damn the boy racers. Damn them all to hell.

I feel sure the bods at Chelsea could advise me on a new hedge. A bonsai perhaps, which needs watering with Chablis every fifteen minutes and grows best if set in dappled shade on a bed of uncut diamonds.

Sunday 25 May 2003

To Boldly Go Where Nobody's Tried a Dumb Record Before

It's starting to look like Australia maintains a modern navy only to pluck hapless British explorers from their tiny upturned boats.

Last week an Aussie frigate sailed thousands of miles to rescue two chaps who were attempting to row across the Indian Ocean. No, I don't know why either, but as far as I can tell, one of them got a headache from a freak wave and decided to call it a day.

And who can forget the epic tale of Tony Bullimore who started to eat himself after his yacht capsized in the Southern Ocean. Luckily, he'd only gnawed his way through half of one hand when *HMAS Adelaide* steamed into view.

It all sounds very *Boy's Own* but the Australian tax-payers are starting to get a bit cross, and I can't say I blame them. Their navy was involved in the recent bout of Middle Eastern fisticuffs and has a torrid time patrolling the waters off Darwin in an endless search for desperate Indonesians who've been drifting on cardboard for fourteen years with nothing to eat but their fingernails.

Then, every fifteen minutes, they have to break off and sail 1,500 miles in rotten weather, and at vast expense, to rescue some weird-beard Englishman who's down to his last Vesta.

The problem is that humans have already climbed the highest mountains and sailed on their own through the wildest and loneliest stretches of ocean. But though the records have gone, the world is still full of Chichesters and Hillarys and Amundsens.

As a result, these people have to think of stupider things to quench their need for a spot of frostbitten glory. So, they insert a few sub-clauses into the record and set off from Margate to become the First Person Ever to Pogo-Stick Round the World – Backwards.

Did you see base camp in the Himalayas last week? It was a smorgasbord of dopamine and lunacy, with people in silly outfits from all four corners of the globe. 'Yes, I'm attempting to be the first Chinese person to climb Everest in a tutu.'

'Oh really. I shall be the second Peruvian ever to go up there in a scuba suit but I'm hoping to be the first not to come back down again.'

Then we have a chap called Pen Hadow. Plainly, it's in his biological make-up to have icicles in his eyes, so he has to go to the Arctic. But what record is left to beat? We've had the first person to drive to the North Pole, the first person to walk to the North Pole unaided and, probably, the first to jog there, from Russia, in a kilt. But Pen wasn't going to be defeated before he'd even set off.

So he pored over the record books and spotted an opening. Eureka! He would become the First Person

Ever to Trek to the Geographic North Pole from Canada, Unaided.

This meant skiing, clambering and swimming through open water, while towing a 300-lb sled. But he made it, a point verified by the tourists who will have watched him arrive from the warmth of their helicopters and their cruise ships.

Sadly, though, he wasn't able to make it back and, as a result, some poor Canadian pilot who was just sitting down to a nice moose sandwich with his family had to effect a daring and spectacular airborne rescue.

This is my biggest beef about explorers today. When Shackleton's boat was crushed by the ice, he didn't think: 'Crikey, it's a bit nippy out. Let's get the Argies on the sat phone and have them bring a destroyer.' No, he ate his dogs, sang some songs, rowed like billy-o and emerged from the event an enduring national hero.

Now compare this with the case of Simon Chalk. Last year he had to be rescued when his rowing boat bumped into a whale. And now he is attempting to become the Youngest Person Ever to Row from Australia to an Island Nobody's Ever Heard Of, On His Own.

I know someone has already rowed the Pacific so I have no idea why we're supposed to get excited about some bloke who's rowing a much shorter distance, and in some style by all accounts. According to the BBC: 'He will run out of drinks on day 85 and after that he will have to survive on water.'

I'm sorry. What drinks? Was he mixing himself a little gin and French after a hard day's tugging?

This sounds like the kind of record I'd like to attempt: The Most Luxurious Crossing of the World's Smallest, Warmest Ocean, Eating Only Quail's Eggs and Celery Salt.

Meanwhile, I have a suggestion for all of you who are only happy when you have gangrene and only feel alive when you're less than an inch from death. Stop messing around in your upturned bathtubs in the southern oceans. If you really have to perform endurance trials at sea, do it near America.

Then when it all goes wrong, it'll be the US Navy who'll come to the rescue.

And if an American naval vessel is employed picking up Mr Scott-Shackleton who was attempting to swim underwater from San Francisco to Tokyo, it won't be able to rain cruise missiles down on whatever unfortunate country George W. Bush has heard of that week.

It's win–win for Mr Templeman-Ffiennes. If he succeeds, he becomes the First Person to Cross the Pacific on a Bicycle. If he fails, he saves the world.

Sunday 8 June 2003

Beckham's Tried, Now It's My Turn to Tame the Fans

If there's any more fighting on the terraces, the England football team will not be allowed to take part in the Euro World Olympic Championship Cup 2004.

This came as a bit of a surprise because I thought football hooliganism had gone away. I thought the stands were all full of families saying things like 'Ooh, look at Michael's dribbling skills' and 'Gosh, have you seen David's new Alice band?'

But it seems not. Things are apparently so bad that President Beckham addressed the nation recently. No, honestly, that's what it said in the papers – that he 'addressed the nation' appealing for calm in the run-up to whatever championship it is that we're going to lose next.

It's a good time then to pause a while and think a little bit about why people fight and how they might be stopped from doing so.

The other day I was staying in a northern town. I shan't say which one because the local newspaper will spend the next six months pillorying me, so let's call it Rotherhullcastlepool.

Anyway, opposite the hotel was a nightclub and outside that was a lengthy queue of people who, despite the chill, appeared to be as-near-as-makes-no-difference naked.

It seemed odd queuing to get into a nightclub at 11 p.m. when, obviously, it was full. And it was going to stay full, surely. Nobody leaves a nightclub at 11, not when the nearest one is 40 miles away in Donfieldgow-on-Trent.

I was wrong. Every few minutes two more lads would come flying out of the door in a flurry of fists and torn T-shirts. After they'd been calmed down by some kicks from the bouncers, two more people were allowed in.

I watched this for a while and began to speculate on what might be causing so many fights in there. Drink? Girls? Drugs? Gangsterism? I think not. I think the root cause of the problem was unintelligence.

I'm told that if all creatures were the same size, the lobster would have the smallest brain. All it knows to do is eat and snap at something if its pint is spilled.

Well, this is what you find in northern nightclubs. Someone looks at your girlfriend, you hit them. Someone looks at you, you hit them. With really stupid creatures, any stimulation whatsoever provokes a lobster response.

My older children have the mental age of eight- and seven-year-olds, because they are eight and seven years old. So they hit each other pretty much constantly. When the boy refuses to give his big sister a Pringle, she doesn't yet have the vocabulary to formulate a reasoned argument. So she whacks him.

We see the same story in America. As a relatively new

country, full of relatively daft people, it doesn't have the wisdom or the experience to construct a sensible response. So when it's prodded, it lashes out with its jets and its aircraft carriers.

I've never hit anyone. I may not have the mind of John Humphrys or the nose of Stephen Fry, but even I, with my six O levels, know that if I punch someone, they will punch me right back. And that, because this will hurt, it's best in a tricky situation to run like hell.

Only once was this not an option. A girlfriend had been pinned against the wall by a wiry, tattooed man whose speech was slurred by a combination of drink and being from Glasgow. He wanted very much for her to kiss him.

So what was I to do? The sensible answer was 'nothing' but I feared a terrible row when we got home so having weighed things up for a while, I tapped the drunken Scotsman on the shoulder and said, as politely as possible: 'Excuse me.'

He whirled round, his eyes full of fire and his hands balled into steel-hard fists. But the blow never came. 'Christ, you're a big bastard,' he said, and ran off. It was the proudest moment of my life.

In fact, I have only ever been hit once. It was a big, rounded, fully formed punch to the side of my head and it was landed by someone who was Greek, right in front of two policemen. Who then arrested me for being beaten up. Like I said. Daft as brushes, the lot of them. But would the Greek have punched me in the first place if nobody had been looking?

Are fights like the light in your fridge? Do they go on when nobody else is there? Or does there have to be an audience to both light the spark and then pull the opponents apart when things turn ugly and the claret starts to flow?

I've just been outside to speak with my builders who know about such things and apparently in all their years they've never heard of what they call a 'one-on-one'. Two blokes, jackets off, fighting to settle something quietly round the back of the pub.

So if the England football team want to avoid trouble at future events they have to play without an audience, live or on television. And it'd probably be for the best if President Beckham, clean living and well meaning though he may be, stops addressing the nation.

In fact it's probably best if he leaves the nation altogether – before someone kicks a boot into his other eye.

Sunday 15 June 2003

The Unhappiest People on Earth?
You'd Never Guess

In a recent survey to find the happiest people in the world, the super-smug Swiss came out on top. Just 3.6 per cent of the population realised that having a punctual bus service and someone else's teeth are not the be all and end all of life and said they were dissatisfied with their lot.

Whatever. The most interesting finding is to be found at the bottom of the table: the country with the most unhappy people.

I would have gone for Niger. I went there once, to a small town in the middle of nowhere called Agadez, and it was pretty damn close to even Lucifer's idea of hell on earth. You could almost taste the hopelessness and smell the despair. There were no crops to tend and no factories to work in.

There was a shower, around which the town had been built, I suppose, and there was a table football game which seemed to amuse the children – even though the ball had been lost long ago.

It was a desperate place but, it seems, somewhere is worse. Finland, perhaps? It's a sensible thought. You are apparently in the First World with your mobile phone and your pretty daughters but you spend all winter being frozen to death and all summer being eaten alive by mosquitoes the size of tractors.

I can't imagine that I would be terribly happy living in Afghanistan, either, though I dare say there is some satisfaction in going to bed thinking: 'Well, at least I wasn't shot today.'

When you come to think about it, the list of countries where you have an excuse to be unhappy is huge. I have never been to that featureless moonscape that's now called Somethingikstan but I can't imagine it's a barrel of laughs. And I'm not sure I would like it in Brazil, either, having to walk around in a thong to demonstrate that I had nothing about my person worth stealing.

Then there's that swathe of misery that stretches along the Kinshasa Highway in the middle of Africa. A land of flies, starvation and HIV.

A land that undermines a British social worker's idea of poverty. However, the poll found that the people who are less satisfied with life than anyone else are . . . drum roll here . . . the Italians.

Oh, now you mention it, it's obvious. Whiling away those long, warm summer evenings in the Tuscan hills with some cheese and a bottle or two of Vernaccia di San Gimignano. *La dolce vita*? It's Italian for 'the ungrateful bastards'.

Even if we poke about in Italy's dark and secret places, we don't find much to complain about. The Mafia has been on the wane for the past ten years, and how can anyone complain about Silvio Berlusconi's alleged corruption when they themselves need a backhander to get out of bed in the morning.

Besides, our prime minister is much worse. He has made a complete hash of everything and now he has started attacking cross-dressers, sacking men for wearing tights in the House of Lords. Despite this and the drizzle and the awful pub food, only 8.5 per cent of us say we're unhappy.

What's more, while extremism is on the rise in Britain, it's now a damp squib in Italy. With immigrants making up just 2.2 per cent of the population there, the far right cannot get much of a toehold and while there are a few communists dotted around here and there, they tend to be one-cal Bolsheviks. Certainly it's been years since there was a really good fist fight in parliament.

Italy's youngsters complain, apparently, about having to live at home until they are 72 but that's because they spend all their money on suits and coffee and Alfa Romeos rather than mortgages.

Of course, I can see that there are drawbacks to life in Italy. It must be annoying to have to post your letters in Switzerland if you want them to stand any chance of arriving, and I would quickly become bored with being killed on the autostrada every day.

Then there's the problem of your wife. One day, you know with absolute certainty, you will come home from work to find that the ravishing beauty you married and said goodbye to that morning is waddling up the street in a black sack with breasts like six sacks of potatoes.

Plus, we think the Germans have no sense of humour, but Hans does at least find some things funny – people falling over on banana skins and Benny Hill, for instance.

Luigi, on the other hand, doesn't even laugh at bottoms. In a country where style is everything and *la bella figura* dictates what you eat, what you wear and how much you drink, there is no room for the helplessness of mirth. As a result, there's no such thing as Eduardo Izzardio or *Torre di Fawlty*.

I don't think this is quite enough, though. Worrying about your wife ballooning and not being able to laugh at your unreliable postal service are not the end of the world, and having a dodgy prime minister is normal.

STOP PRESS: I've just read the result of another survey which says Britain is one of the most dishonest countries in the world. So when 91.5 per cent of us said we were happy, plainly we were lying.

Sunday 22 June 2003

Welcome to Oafsville: It's Any Town Near You

The other night a man from the Campaign to Protect Rural England went on the news to say that housing estates in Ledbury are just the same as estates everywhere else and that all traces of local character are being lost.

'Look,' he said, pointing at the executive homes over his shoulder, 'we could be anywhere from Welwyn Garden City to Milton Keynes.'

'Pah!' I scoffed, reaching for the remote control. 'What's he want? All houses in Somerset to be made from mead and freshly carbonated village idiots? And all houses in Cheshire to be built out of gold and onyx?'

I agree that Bryant and Barratt charge through the countryside with the destructive force of a double-barrelled shotgun, and I welcome any move that eats into their profit margins. If they are forced to make houses in Barnsley out of coal, that's fine by me.

But having spent the week on a mammoth tour of England, I can assure you that there are far bigger problems to be addressed. I would go so far as to say that today provincial Britain is probably one of the most depressing places on earth.

Of course, there are worse places, places where you can starve to death or be eaten by flies. But this is a wealthy country with many widescreen television sets, and that's what makes it all so depressing: the sense that it could be so much better.

It's not the villages or the countryside that are wrong. It's the towns, with their pedestrian precincts and the endless parade of charity shops and estate agents.

At night boys, with their baggy trousers and their big shoes, scream up and down the high street in their souped-up Vauxhall Novas. There is nothing you want to see. Nothing you want to do.

You wade knee-deep through a sea of discarded styrofoam trays smeared with bits of last night's horseburger to your overheated chintzy hotel where, in exchange for £75, they give you a room where you can't sleep because of the constant background hum of people coupling or being sick outside.

It's almost as though every council in the land has become so engrossed with their war on the car that they spend all their time and money on speed humps and traffic-calming pots of geraniums. They seem to have lost sight of what the town is for: shopping, chatting, being a pack animal.

There are exceptions, usually towns and cities with universities, such as Oxford, but for the most part urban Britain is utterly devoid of any redeeming feature whatsoever.

And that's before we get to the people. Who are they, with their faces like pastry and their legs like sides of beef? And what on earth do they say to the barber to end up with such stupid hair?

They come from nothing, live a life enlivened only

by a twice-yearly visit to some hairdresser who takes the mickey, and then they die so quietly that they're not even remembered with a plaque on a park bench.

I'm not kidding. In the Third World you will see hopelessness etched onto people's faces but in provincial Britain it's gormlessness.

In the papers and at your house people discuss the euro and Iraq. But you get the sense that in Britain's town centres they simply don't care about anything. They drink, they eat, they mate, then they die. They might as well be spiders.

Scottish Courage, a brewery, is to be commended for launching a new type of drink to ease the misery. It's a bottle of Kronenbourg sold with a shot of absinthe, a bright green hallucinogen that is 50% proof.

Banned by many countries throughout the civilised world, though not the Czech Republic and Britain, it was a favourite tipple for all the maddest artists. Van Gogh was reported to have drunk the stuff before cutting off his ear. Oscar Wilde said: 'After the first glass, you see things as you wish they were. After the second, you see things as they are not.'

This then is the perfect solution for life in provincial Britain today. One glass and you imagine you're not in Hastings at all. After the second you imagine that you are in fact in St Tropez and that the monosyllabic fizzy-haired girl you've just pulled won't give you something nasty to remember her by. After the third, your hair starts to look normal.

Experts say that mixing lager and absinthe is like drinking Night Nurse and Ovaltine and that its sole purpose is to get you drunk. So what? I see nothing wrong with that.

All over northern Europe people drink to get drunk, but in Reykjavik, the biggest drinking city anywhere, they don't come out of the clubs for a vomit and a fight.

In Stockholm the city centre is not buried under a styrofoam mountain every morning.

I do not understand why this should be so here. Maybe, deep down, there's a sense that Britain had fulfilled its obligations to the world by 1890 and that now we're like a nation of spent matches, serving out our time in IT or by changing the crabby sheets at the local overheated hotel.

Whatever, I certainly have no answers. But building speed humps certainly won't help. And nor, I suspect, will worrying about the gable ends on houses in Ledbury.

Sunday 29 June 2003

If Only My Garden Grew As Well As the Hair in My Ears

There are many signs of middle age: hair growing out of your ears, a waistband that will not stop expanding no matter what you put in your mouth and an increasing bewilderment at the noises made by Radio 1.

But the seminal moment when you know for sure that you have become old is when you look out of your bedroom window and say: 'Ooh good, it's raining.' This means you are more interested in your plants looking good than getting a tan and looking good yourself.

For 43 years I have sneezed my way through the British summer, swigging from bottles of Piriton and gorging on handfuls of Zirtec. But hay fever has never dampened my enthusiasm for those lazy days in the garden, listening to men surge by on their motorbikes.

Mainly this is because I've never really had a garden in the accepted sense of the word. Too much sun and too little chalk in the soil have little or no effect on rubble and weeds. Now, however, with a veritable forest growing out of my ears, I have become interested in maybe having a herbaceous border here and a weeping pear there. So I was interested to read about the olive trees of southern Italy. In the war so many were chopped down for firewood that the government imposed a ban, saying they could not be uprooted without permission from Mussolini.

When the war ended the law was never repealed, so the trees grew older and older.

They became fat and tufts of hair began to appear from their knots. What's more, the fruit they produced became worse and worse to the point where it could be used only in paraffin lamps.

Then along came Charlie Dimmock. Suddenly, everyone in northern Europe decided they would like a century-old olive tree in their garden. A booming black market was the result, with Bavarian bankers paying up to £3,500 for a 'gnarled designer' tree to enliven their Munich roof terrace.

Inevitably the tree huggers are up in arms and, for once, I'm with them. What's the point of paying £3,500 for something that I guarantee will be dead within six months?

This is the one thing I've learnt during my short spell as a gardener: everything dies. Two weeks ago I spent £500 on a selection of plants for my conservatory after the last lot were killed by scale insect. On Sunday I went to London for the day, and when I came home at night it looked as if the American Air Force had been through the place with some Agent Orange and napalm. 'You should have left the windows open,' say the experts. So you leave the windows open, which means your plants survive. But, sadly, your video recorder and PlayStation do not.

Because someone with a Ford Fiesta haircut and baggy trousers will walk in and help themselves.

Things are no better outside. Keen to have instant results, I laid some turf the other day and my life became consumed by where the sprinkler was and where it needed to be next. Please God, I would wail as the sun girded its loins for another blistering day, have mercy. But there was no mercy, no rain, and now my new turf looks like that sisal matting in the Fired Earth brochures.

You sit in the garden only when it's sunny, but you can't relax because you know the sun is a 5-trillion-ton nuke and by the time you go indoors at night every living thing out there, except the thistles, will be dead.

I bought some plants with red flowers which stood tall and so erect that they seemed to have been fertilised with Viagra. After one day in the sunshine they had keeled over and nothing I have tried will make them stand up again. I've watered them, not watered them, read them poetry, played them Whitney Houston records and shown them pictures of the Prince of Wales. But it's hopeless.

I had a tree surgeon round yesterday to talk about the mature trees that are dotted around the garden. Unbelievably, I have to maintain these things in case some village kids try to climb them and a branch breaks. That's true, that is.

His report was shocking. The lime is dying quite fast. The poplars are pretty much dead already and the sycamore, with a trunk that's fully 12 feet in circumference, has some kind of incurable rot. So it will spend the next ten years dropping boughs on passing motorcyclists who'll then sue me for negligence.

He has stripped it right back so now it's virtually naked. But even this tree porn has failed to perk the wilting red plants back into life. The oak? That was doing quite well. I think in the past seven years it had shot up by a millionth of an inch. But it's hard to be sure because the other day a cow ate it. That's nothing, though. The honeysuckle has strangled the cherry. Clematis has suffocated the copper beech and ivy has asphyxiated one of the silver birches. It's like *The Killing Fields* out there.

What about my latest purchase? Six weeks ago I wrote about failing to find a statue of Hitler killing an otter at the Chelsea Flower Show. Now I've bought a lump of Canadian driftwood which, I'm assured, died 400 years ago.

Knowing my luck, the damn thing will come back to life.

Sunday 6 July 2003

Men, You Have Nothing to FEAR But Acronyms

Thursday should have been a great day. I was with the Royal Green Jackets in a small German village called Copehill Down which is to be found thirteen miles from anywhere in the middle of Salisbury Plain.

I was part of an eight-man team charged with the task of storming a well-defended house, shooting everyone inside and getting out again in under fifteen minutes.

The rules were simple. I was to stick with my buddy unless he got wounded in which case I was to leave him behind. Marvellous. None of that soppy American marine nonsense in the British forces.

So, dolled up like Action Man, I had the latest SA80 assault rifle slung over my right shoulder and, in my trouser pockets, a clutch of grenades. I was going to kick ass, unleash a hail of hot lead and do that American war-film thing where I point at my eyes, then point at a wood and then make a black power sign, for no reason.

Unfortunately, things went badly. They had asked me to bring along the explosives which would blow a hole in the side of the house, but I forgot, which meant we all had to climb through a window. It turns out that it's amazingly easy to shoot someone when they're doing this.

I was shot the first time in the sitting room and again

on the stairs. Then some burly commandos picked me up and shoved me through a trap door into the attic.

Well, when I say 'through', this is not entirely accurate. My embarrassingly significant stomach became wedged in the hole, which meant my head and upper torso were in the loft with three of the enemy while the rest of me and my gun were on the landing below. And believe me, it's even easier to shoot someone when they're in this position than when they're climbing through a window.

Happily, because everyone was firing blanks, I wasn't really killed. Although my buddy probably wished I had been a few moments later when I threw a grenade at him, blowing most of his legs off.

The problems with doing this sort of thing are many. First, we were all wearing exactly the same clothes and full warpaint so my buddy looked like everyone else.

And second, there are so many levers on an SA80 that every time I wanted fully automatic fire, or to engage the laser sights, the magazine fell out.

But worse than this is the army's insistence on talking almost exclusively in acronyms. Throughout the firefight the house had echoed to the sound of mumbo-jumbo, none of which made any sense at all. 'DETCON WOMBAT' shouted someone into my earpiece. 'FOOTLING REVERB' yelled someone else. Rat-a-tat-tat barked the enemy's AK47 and beep went my earpiece to signify I had been shot again.

Things were not explained in the debrief. This, said the colour sergeant, had been FIBUA (Fighting in

Built-Up Areas) and we had done FISH (Fighting in Someone's House). Clarkson, he didn't need to point out, had been a FLOS (Fat Lump of S★★★).

Needless to say, this was all being filmed for television and my director was thrilled. 'It was great,' she said. 'Good stuff for OOV. All we need now is a PTC or two, a BCU, then an MCU and we're done.'

Done we were, so I asked the colonel for directions out of Germany and back into Wiltshire. 'Sure,' he said, starting out well. 'You go right at Parsonage Farm, right at the church . . .' and then he blew it: 'and you'll be at the Vetcom Spectre Viperfoobarcomsatdefcon.'

'You mean the exit,' I said.

'Yes,' he replied, and in doing so exposed the lie that acronyms were invented to save time. They weren't. They were invented to make you feel part of a club and to exclude, in a sneery mocking sort of way, those who aren't.

How many times have we seen the president in American films ordering a man in green clothes to go to Defcon 3? Hundreds. And do you know what – I still have no idea what this means, or which way the numbering goes. Even now, if someone told me to go to Defcon 1, I wouldn't know whether to launch the nukes or cancel lunch.

The trouble is that everyone's at it. After my day of FISH I drove to London and hosted an awards ceremony for the world's top bankers. The organisers had written a speech which I delivered to the best of my ability even though I had no idea what any of it meant. It was full of

FIRCS and CUSTODIES and NECRS, and to make things even more complicated I'd say UBS had had a good year on the FIRM and everyone would fall about laughing. I felt excluded, an outsider. Which is the point of course.

When someone uses an acronym they want you to ask what they mean so they can park an incredulous look on their face: 'What, you don't know?' Then they will look clever when they have to explain.

A word of warning, though. Don't try this on television or you will hear the presenter ask the cameraman to fit the strawberry filter. This is a device reserved for crashing bores who've driven a long way to appear on the box and who don't want to be told that they're not interesting enough. It means: 'Set the camera up. But don't bother turning it on.'

Sunday 13 July 2003

Red Sky at Night, Michael Fish's Satellite is On Fire

I rang the Meteorological Office last week and asked something which in the whole 149 years of the service it has never been asked before. 'How come,' I began, 'your weather forecasts are so accurate these days?'

Sure, there have been complaints from the tourist industry in recent months that the weathermen 'sex up' bulletins, skipping over the sunny skies anticipated in England, Scotland and Wales and concentrating instead on some weather of mass destruction that they are juicily expecting to find on Rockall.

That's as maybe, but the fact is this: weather reports in the past were rubbish, works of fiction that may as well have been written by Alistair MacLean. And now they aren't.

We were told that the heatwave would end last Tuesday, and it did. We were told that Wednesday would be muggy and thundery as hell, and it was. When I woke up on Thursday, without opening the curtains I knew to put on a thick shirt because they had been saying for days that it would be wet, cold and windy.

It is not just 24-hour predictions, either. Now you are told with alarming accuracy what the weather will be like in two or even three days' time. So how are the bods in the Met Office's new Exeter headquarters doing this?

The man who answered the telephone seemed a bit surprised by the pleasantness of my question. But once he had climbed back into his chair and removed the tone of incredulity from his voice, he began a long and complicated explanation about modern weather forecasting.

At least I think it was about weather forecasting. It was so difficult to follow that, if I am honest, it could have been his mother's recipe for baked Alaska.

In a nutshell, it seems that they get hourly reports from meteorological observation points all over the world. These are then added to the findings from a low-orbit satellite that cruises round the world every 107 minutes, at a height of 800 miles, measuring wave heights.

Other satellites looking at conditions in the troposphere and the stratosphere chip in with their data and then you add sugar, lemon and milk and feed the whole caboodle into a Cray supercomputer that is capable of making about eleventy billion calculations a second.

This system, soon to be updated with an even cleverer computer, has been operational since the middle of the 1990s, which does beg a big question: what was the point of weather forecasting before it came along? Everyone was jolly cross with Michael Fish when he didn't see the 1987 storm coming. But it turns out that he had no satellites and no computers, just a big checked jacket.

Big checked jackets are no good at predicting the

weather. Nor, it seems, are those mud 'n' cider bods who tramp around Somerset with big earlobes and a forked twig. Back in the spring a gnarled old Cotswold type told me that because of the shape of the flies and the curl of the cow pats we were in for a lousy July. My gleaming red nose testifies to the fact that he was wrong.

Then you have people who say you can tell when rain is coming because the cows are lying down. Not so. According to my new friend at the Met Office, cows lie down because they are tired.

There are some pointers. Swallows fly differently when there is thunder about, and high clouds have tails pointing to the north-west when you are about to get wet.

Furthermore, red sky at night signifies that hot, dusty air is coming while red sky in the morning shows it has gone away.

However, using the natural world as a pointer is mainly useless because it is good for showing only what weather there is now, which you know, or what is coming in a minute. Pine cones, crows and especially otters do not know what pressure systems are prevalent in the Atlantic, or where they are going.

Then I said to the man from the Met, what if a low-pressure area suddenly veers north for no reason? The computer must occasionally get it wrong. It does, apparently, but there are six senior weather forecasters at the Met Office who decide whether to believe it or not.

Now that has to be one of the ballsiest jobs in Britain today. The most powerful computer is telling you that two and two is five. And you have to say, 'No, it isn't.'

There is, however, a worrying downside to the accuracy levels of this man and machine combo.

The British are known throughout the world for moaning about the weather. It is one of our defining national characteristics. It is not the variety we hate, though. That is a good thing. It's the unpredictability. When you turn up at royal Ascot in a pair of wellingtons and the sun shines all day, it is annoying. And it is the same story if your summer dress gets all soaked and see-through at Henley.

What happens if the unpredictability is removed from the equation? If you know what the weather will be like on Tuesday you'll be able to organise a barbecue knowing that the sun will be out. Then what will you talk about?

Inadvertently, those computer geeks are unpicking the very fabric of everything that makes us British.

Sunday 20 July 2003

I Wish I'd Chosen Marijuana and Biscuits Over Real Life

Right. You've got to take me seriously this morning because I am no longer a jumped-up motoring journalist with a head full of rubbish. I am now a doctor. I have a certificate.

Yes, Brunel University has given me an honorary degree, or an *honoris causa*, as we scholars like to call it. So now I am a doctor. I can mend your leg and give you a new nose. I am qualified to see your wife naked and design your next fridge freezer. I think I might even have some letters after my name.

Sadly, they don't send doctorates through the post. So last Monday I had to go to the historic Wembley Conference Centre near the North Circular where they gave me a robe and floppy hat that made me look like a homosexual.

The whole event was designed to run like clockwork. I had been told weeks beforehand about every last detail, including how many steps there were between the entrance and the stage.

I knew why of course. I'd be entering as a normal man, a thicky, and I had to be told there were 21 steps or I might stop halfway, thinking I'd made it.

On the way out, as a fully fledged doctor of everything,

there were no instructions at all. It just said 'procession out'.

In between, a man in a robe read out half a million names, most of which seem to have been a collection of letters plucked from a Scrabble bag, and the students filed past the chancellor, an endless succession of beaming brown and yellow faces, collected their degrees and set off into the world.

I was deeply, properly, neck-reddeningly jealous. Dammit, I thought, sitting there in my Joseph coat and my Elton hat. Why didn't I do this?

You should never regret any experience, but my God, it is possible to regret missing out on one. And that's what I did, 25 years ago when I decided there were better things to do at school than read Milton.

I used his books as bog rolls and as a result lost my shot at paradise: university.

Yes, things have worked out pretty well since – they even gave me an honorary degree for dangling around under Brunel's suspension bridge. Yet there is a chink in the smoothness of it all. Well, more of a chip really, on my shoulder.

I am sure a university education wouldn't have made the slightest difference to my professional life. From what I can gather, students spend their three years after school either on an island off Australia pretending to study giant clams, or being pushed down the high street in a bed. Or drunk.

Certainly I learnt more in my three years on the

Rotherham Advertiser than some of those students who were at Wembley on Monday.

One, I noted, had studied the ramifications of having sex in prison while another had spent her time looking at the correlation between life in Bhutan and life in Southall.

But I'm no fool. Not now anyway. And I know that even the silliest university course is more fun than putting on a tie every morning and working for a living.

When I was nineteen, I was trawling the suburbs of Rotherham for stories, listening to fat women telling me their kiddies' heads were full of insect eggs and that the council should be doing something about it.

Oh sure, I was paid £17 a week, which covered my petrol and ties. But I was acutely aware that half of my earnings was being taken away and given to students who were spending it on marijuana and biscuits. While you were settling down for an evening's arguing at the debating society, I was poring over my South Yorkshire/English translation book, desperately trying to work out what Councillor Ducker was on about.

While you were being bollocked for missing your eighteenth lecture in a row, I was being hauled over the coals for misreading my shorthand notes and as a result getting my report of the inquest disastrously wrong. And all you had to do to set things right was sleep with your tutor. I could not solve my problem by sleeping with the libel judge.

When you've been educated by the university of life you arrive at the top completely worn out.

Real university, on the other hand, gives you a leg up so everything is less exhausting.

Then there is the question of friends. I know people who went to university with Stephen Fry and Richard Curtis and Boris Johnson. Let's not forget that Eric Idle, John Cleese and Graham Chapman were at Cambridge together, and what must a night out with that lot have been like? More fun, I should imagine, than a night out with the friends you made while stocking shelves at Safeway.

Let me try to intellectualise it for you. At the beginning of the ceremony in Wembley the Vice-Chancellor of Brunel addressed the audience saying that there are 50 institutions in Europe that go back more than a thousand years.

There's the Catholic Church, the parliaments of Britain, Iceland and the Isle of Man and a few quasi-governmental organisations in Italy.

All the rest are universities. They work. And I missed out. And to my dying day I shall regret it.

Sunday 27 July 2003

I've been to Paradise . . . It was an Absolute Pain

'No.' That's what I said when the producers of a programme about the jet engine asked if I'd like to fly round the world in five days.

'Yes.' That's what I said when they pointed out that we'd be breaking the journey with a day on the beach in somewhere called Moorea, which is a small tropical island five minutes from Tahiti.

On paper, French Polynesia sounds like one of the most exotic idylls anywhere on earth, a collection of 120 or so islands dotted over an area of the south Pacific that's the same size as Europe. In reality, it takes 24 hours to get there and it's not worth the bother.

At the airport everyone from the customs man to the bus driver gave me a necklace of flowers, so that by the time I arrived at the hotel and conference centre I looked like a human garden centre and had a spine the shape of an oxbow lake.

Here, after they'd given me another necklace or two, they wanted to know about breakfast: not what I wanted, but whether I'd like it delivered to my room in a canoe.

And therein lies the heart of the problem with all these pointy lumps of volcanic residue that were pretty much a secret until the jet engine came along. It doesn't matter whether you're talking about Mauritius or the Maldives,

Tahiti or the Seychelles. They are all the same: completely overdone.

All of them are advertised in the brochures with a picture of what I swear is the same palm tree. You must have seen it: the horizontal one, wafting its fronds gently over the turquoise waters and white sand of pretty well everywhere.

Then there are the hotels, with their increasingly idiotic ways of giving you a taste of life on a tropical island.

This means sharing your bath with half a hundredweight of petals and finding your bog roll folded into the shape of a rose every morning and having a monogrammed Hobie Cat moored to your own manservant. Is that what it was like for Robinson Crusoe? How do you know? Because when you're there, one thing's for sure, you won't set foot outside the hotel grounds.

To complete the picture, the staff are dolled up in a ludicrous facsimile of what once, perhaps, might have been the national dress. Even the blokes in Tahiti had to wear skirts, and to complete their humiliation they had to walk up and down the superheated sand all day in bare feet.

Unless of course they were trying to deliver a mountain of bacon and eggs, in a canoe, on a choppy sea, without letting it blow away or go cold or fall into the water.

Small wonder they behaved like everything was too much trouble. Give the poor bastards some shoes, for crying out loud. And some strides.

Did I mention the dolphin? As a unique selling point

the boys in Tahiti had caught themselves a big grey beasty which spent all day on its back, in a lagoon, being pawed by overweight American women with preposterous plastic tits and unwise G-string bikini bottoms. 'Would you like to see his penis?' asked the man in a skirt when I climbed into the water.

No. What I'd like to do is spear you through the heart with a harpoon and let the miserable thing have a taste of freedom. But instead I tickled its belly and whispered into its ear: 'Call that a penis, acorn crotch.'

Thinking that this sort of thing is giving you a taste of life on a tropical island is as silly as thinking you can get a taste of beef from licking a cow. On a real tropical island, like Tom Hanks in *Castaway*, you have to smash your own teeth out with ice skates and talk to footballs, and there are insects, huge articulated things with the head and upper torso of a hornet and the rear end of a wolf.

I stayed at one hotel, can't remember where, where they made the locals trample about in the flower beds all day with Volkswagen Beetle engines on their backs spraying the bushes with insecticide.

Occasionally one of the poor chaps would gas himself to death, or catch his skirt in the machinery, and have to be carted off. But soon there'd be another in his place. And for what purpose? To sanitise paradise? It didn't work. So far as I could see, the spray seemed to make the insects a little bit bigger.

Don't be fooled by the sun either. It may look nice in the pictures, dipping its feet into the sea after a hard day warming the solar system, but in reality it'll cause you to sit in the shade all day until you look like a stick of forced rhubarb. And it'll melt the glue in the spine of your book, allowing the last ten pages to blow away just before you get there.

There's no respite at night either. You won't be able to sleep with the air con on, it'll be too noisy. And you won't be able to sleep with it off because then all you'll hear is the squeals of the honeymoon couple in the authentic bungalow next door.

Only once have I been to a tropical beach that was completely unmolested. It was in Vietnam and it was perfect. Except that after twenty minutes or so I wanted a girl in a skimpy ao dai to bring me a cold Coke.

And there's the thing. We dream the tropical dream. But we're built to live in Dewsbury.

Sunday 31 August 2003

Eureka, I've Discovered a Cure for Science

A report in the paper last week said that the world is running out of scientists as pupils opt for 'easy' subjects like media studies rather than difficult ones like the effect of fluorocarbons on methionylglutaminylarginyltyrosyl glutamylserylleucylphenylalanylalanylglutaminylleucyl lysylglutamylarginyllysylglutamylglycylalanylphenyl anylvalylprolylphenylalanylvalylthreonylleucylglycy laspartylprolylglycylisoleucylutamylglutaminylserylleu cyllysylisoleucylaspartylthreonylleucyl . . .

Sadly, I shall have to call a halt to the actual name of this natty little protein at this point because I'm paid by the word. And I don't want to get to the end of the column having written only one. It illustrates the point neatly, though. Which would you rather do? Hang around in Soho, drinking skinny lattes with Graham Norton, or emigrate to somewhere like Durham and spend your life teaching hydrogen how to speak?

That's not such a silly idea because underneath the report about a shortage of scientists was another which said that a professor of acoustics at Salford University has proved that, contrary to popular belief, a duck's quack does echo.

Though only faintly.

Who gives a stuff? Apparently, the professor in

question was trying to solve the problem of echoey public address systems in churches and stadiums. But quite what the duck has to do with this, I have no idea. I mean, what's he going to do? Give the vicar's job to a mallard?

Elsewhere in the world, other scientists have been monitoring 25 sites in America's Great Basin. And they've found that the pika, a small and useless relative of the rabbit, is not coping as well as might be hoped with global warming. Oh dear.

Here at home, scientists have discovered that children who gorge on fizzy drinks in the morning have the reaction times of a 70-year-old. Only, I should imagine, if the fizzy drink in question is champagne.

Ooh, here's a good one. Two British teams of medical researchers have generated a human cell. Sounds spooky, so should we be worried? Not really. They say this is the first step to growing replacement livers, but this seems a trifle farfetched since there is no way of telling a cell what to become. You may hope for a liver and end up with an ear. Only God can decide, and thanks to science all his representatives on earth are soon to be replaced with ducks.

I know it must be depressing when Greenpeace rolls around on your important and juicy discoveries, like GM food, but why have you spent so long determining that women who take pain-killers at the time of conception are more likely to miscarry? Even you, in your freezing lab, must realise that conception cannot happen unless something takes the headache away first.

It gets worse. In America, scientists have spent $1.2 m (£750,000) of public money trying to prove that conservatives are nutty. In Canada, they've studied 2,000 Pisceans and determined they're not all wetties who are still crying over *Born Free*. And in Holland, they're examining a prehistoric slug that has no brain or sex organs to see if it's some kind of evolutionary missing link. Unlikely, if it doesn't have a penis or a womb.

For heaven's sake people, where's the next Concorde? Where's the pill we can live on instead of food, and what about the dog in a space suit we were promised by Valerie Singleton? Put your ducks away and do something useful.

With this in mind, I went to see Professor Kevin Warwick in the cybernetics department of Reading University last week. He has built what looks like a radio-controlled car but in fact it's a robot that has the intelligence, he says, of a wasp.

If you turn its power supply off, it will look for more, in the same way that a wasp will look for food. And it can be programmed to buzz around your head all day too.

Warwick is so obsessed with artificial intelligence he recently had a plug surgically implanted in his nervous system. Then he hooked himself up to a computer so, as he moved his hand in New York, a robotic hand back home in Reading moved too.

And his point is? Well, I had no idea until he told me that he'd had his wife's central nervous system hooked up to the web too. Now that . . . that boggles the mind.

The possibilities of feeling what your wife feels, and vice versa, have to be one of the most exciting breakthroughs since . . . since . . . ever. And imagine being tapped into the brain of a computer at the same time. Working on the G-spot and a system to beat the gee-gees simultaneously.

My enthusiasm was curbed somewhat when Warwick explained that a man/machine hybrid might not be satisfied with the governorship of California and could, perhaps, decide one day to wreak a trail of destruction across the world. I suggested that machines are never scary because you can always turn them off but he smiled the smile of a brainbox and said, simply: 'Really? How do you turn the internet off then?'

If he has a point then maybe a dearth of scientists over the coming years is no bad thing. Because it would only take one to put down his duck for five minutes and destroy the planet.

Sunday 14 September 2003

Why the Booker Shortlist Always Loses the Plot

A couple of months ago I wrote about books here. It was the time of the Hay Festival, which is like Glastonbury only quieter, more dusty and without Rolf Harris.

Jilly Cooper had hit out at the intellectual snobbery of it all. 'There are two categories of writers,' she said at the time, 'Jeffrey Archer and me, who long and long for a kind word in the *Guardian*, and the others who get all the kind words and long to be able to do what Jeffrey and I do.'

Wise words. But not wise enough, it seems, for the panel of judges who selected this year's Man Booker Prize shortlist.

Joint favourite to win is a book called *Brick Lane* by Monica Ali, which is centred on the letters exchanged between two sisters, one of whom lives in Bangladesh and one who came to London for an arranged marriage.

Now I haven't read it, and I never will, but I think we can be fairly sure that neither of the sisters will have a torrid affair with an unsuitable rogue called Rupert.

So what of the other joint favourite? That's from Margaret Atwood, who has got her, I suspect, voluminous knickers in a tangle over Monsanto and its GM food development. *Oryx and Crake*, her book, is unlikely to be a comedy.

It's also worth mentioning Damon Galgut's *The Good Doctor*, which is about a young medic who finds himself posted to a tribal homeland in South Africa. Is he dive-bombed by F-15 fighters? Is the *Nimitz* sunk? Don't hold your breath.

I have just finished a book by Philip Roth, one of the most revered highbrow authors, and it was astonishing. It's about the owner of a glove factory in New Jersey whose daughter came off the rails a bit.

I ploughed on through page after page of undeniably beautiful prose dying to know if he'd get his daughter back. But all I got was more and more agonising until it just stopped.

It's almost as though Roth rang the publishers and asked: 'How long would you like my next novel to be?' And when they said 250 pages, he said, 'Oh good, I've finished.'

Before this, I read *Gulag* by Anne Applebaum, which was mainly a letter to other people who've written about the Soviet camps, saying they were all wrong. Wrong, do you hear.

But worst of all was *Stupid White Men* by the Stupid White Man himself, Michael Moore.

After the first chapter – an interesting account of how George Bush stole the presidency – it degenerated into an adolescent rant from a student bedsit, *circa* 1982. Thatcher, Thatcher, Thatcher. Big companies. Thatcher. Rainforests.

Governments would rather spend their money on another bomber than education, and why do we fear black men when every bit of suffering in our lives has a Caucasian face attached to it?

He droned on and on and I couldn't take anything he said seriously because in the introduction, before the eco-friendly, power-to-the-people garbage really started to splash onto the page, he criticised the British for privatising 'formerly well-run public entities' – like the rail network.

What? British Rail? Well run? You stupid, fat, four-eyed, grinning, bearded imbecile. He even admitted that he dropped out of college because he couldn't find any-where to park. You should have gone on the train, if you love them so much.

I could heap scorn on Moore until hell freezes over – but back to my point. A book needs more than beautiful sentence construction, a left-wing take and wry observa-tion. It needs, more than anything else, a story. With a story, you have the most powerful of emotions: hope.

You 'hope' Clint Thrust manages to abseil from his Apache gunship successfully and that the third world war is averted. You 'hope' that the heroine meets the hero on the bridge at midnight and they all live happily ever after. You 'hope' that the dream to live in Provence works out.

Sure, I got plenty of hope from Philip Roth. I spent the entire time hoping the glove maker would get his daughter back, but it was dashed by the sudden appear-ance of the ISBN number.

In *Stupid White Men* I hoped the author would fall out of a tall building, but that never happened either.

My wife reads books the size of Agas about women in beekeeper hats who spend 50 years in Peru looking for a lost bracelet. Man Booker books, in other words.

Sometimes I snatch them away and ask: 'What do you hope happens next?' and I always get the same answer: 'Nothing really.'

She can take a year to read something, whereas I like a book that becomes more important in my life than life itself.

When I was in the middle of *Red Storm Rising* by Tom Clancy – which was not selected for the Man Booker shortlist – you could have taken my liver out and fed it to the dog. And I wouldn't have noticed.

Which brings me to *Yellow Dog*, by Martin Amis. It's awful, apparently. Reading it, said Tibor Fischer, the novelist, who reviewed it in the *Daily Telegraph*, was like your favourite uncle being caught masturbating in the school playground.

His views were shared by the Man Booker judges who have left it out of 'the final six'. I bet it's fabulous.

Sunday 28 September 2003

Look in the Souvenir Shop and Weep for England

Picture the scene. We were in France having lunch at Club 55 on the beach in St Tropez and I was explaining to my children just how good the French are at cheese and wine.

And then it happened. Having tried the Brie and declared it to be delicious, my nine-year-old daughter looked up and, out of nowhere, asked the most imposs-ible question I've ever faced. 'Daddy,' she said, 'what are the English good at?'

Now I've been ready for some time for her to say: 'I know I came out of Mummy's tummy but how did I get in there in the first place?' I've been preparing for that one. But: 'What are the English good at?' It took me so completely by surprise that I suddenly felt the need to shove a fish's head into her mouth.

'Well,' I stammered. 'We, er . . . we're good at . . .' For some extraordinary reason Harold Shipman's name came into my head. 'Murdering people,' I suggested. Well we are. We've even started exporting our mur-derers. But I think that in a world murdering league, sinister Belgium is still at No. 1.

I had a quick canter round all the usual suspects: football, cricket, tennis, motor racing and so on, and could come up with nothing. So I moved into the world of innovation and again drew a blank. Our big polythene balloon tore. Our Eurofighter doesn't work if it's chilly. Our trains are not quite as fast as they were before the Second World War when they were named after ducks such as the mallard.

I'm having a crisis about being English at the moment. I was in Berlin last week, the day after Mr Blair had been to see Schroder and Chirac about Iraq, and it was strange walking around the Fatherland apologising to everyone for my country's conduct in the war.

Speaking of which, did you know that *HMS Invincible* has to limp around the world on one engine because the Royal Navy cannot afford the fuel for two? How frightening is that?

But this is symptomatic of a serious problem. Beneath the surface, everything is half cocked. Have you, for instance, inadvertently walked through a staff-only door into some back staircase in any public building? It's unbelievable. Miles of institutional paint dragging plaster off the walls. Huge puddles on the floor, some of which smell of rain and some of which don't. Unshaded light bulbs smeared with melted moths from the 1940s. Broken hinges. Notice boards bearing news of retirement parties. Tick if you want to go. No one has.

On Thursday night I watched a fabulous programme about the building of London's sewers. They were constructed in 1856 and have been almost unmaintained ever since. There are, apparently, 186,000 miles of sewers in Britain and in 2002 only 241 miles were mended or replaced.

British Airways is run by an Australian and the English football team is managed by a Swede. Vodafone, Lloyds TSB and the British bid to run the Olympics are now all being run by Yanks. And according to my friends in the City that's now almost exclusively American too.

To get an idea of the scale of the problem, next time you're passing through Terminal 1 at Heathrow check out the souvenir shop, the last chance visitors have to take home a taste of England.

Every airport has one of these. In Detroit, Ford, GM and Motown all run gift shops where you can buy toy cars and posters of Martha Reeves. In Iceland you can buy a nice jumper or a book about waterfalls. In Barbados they do a selection of hot sauces. In Canada they'll sell you a cute dead seal. 'Squeeze its tummy and real blood spurts out of the wound on its head.'

In New York I bought a limited-edition plastic statue of a fireman carrying a buddy through what looks like some chips and ketchup but is in fact bits of the Trade Center. It's called *Red Hats of Courage*.

But at Heathrow all you can get is a flavour of what Britain used to be. The reality is that today's bobby wears a flak jacket and doesn't venture onto the beat without a belt full of mustard gas. But at the airport shop you're offered a teddy bear dressed like Dixon of Dock Green.

Can you imagine the gift shop at Charles de Gaulle offering visitors dolls in berets with onions round their necks? Or the Australians selling bears in convict suits with chains round their feet?

Here, you half expect to find Winston Churchill

dressed up as a beefeater and a talking Sir Walter Raleigh doll in a London taxi. 'Awight guv. 'Ave a fag. Cor lummy.'

Then there's the Queen. How many other countries try to sell tourists crockery featuring a picture of their head of state? A Berlusconi bowl? A Putin plate? I don't think so.

Here, though, they were obviously so desperate to fill the shelves with something – anything – that they will even sell you a plastic Union Jack. How desperate is that? Even Luxembourg doesn't have to resort to selling you a flag.

But of course if the gift shop wanted to represent England today accurately, it'd be tough. Everyone would be going home with a Harold Shipman mug.

Sunday 5 October 2003

Eton – It's Worse than an Inner-City Comprehensive

Oliver Letwin announced last week that he would rather beg on the streets than send his children to an inner-city state school. He is an old Etonian.

Predictably, every whining, thin-lipped, pasty-faced, shapeless socialist from one end of Haringey to the other is on the radio moaning and groaning and generally having angst. 'Oh, it's not fair,' they wail. Damn right. It's not fair either that you've got a face like a slapped spaniel. But that's life, loser. Get used to it.

Actually, I don't think old Etonian Oliver went far enough. There is no end to the things I would do to keep my children out of an inner-city state school. I'd rent my car to a minicab firm, my bottom to an internet downloader and my spare room to a family of Azerbaijanis.

Nothing, nothing annoys me more than people who sacrifice their children on the altar of political ideals. The notion that you would send your kids to a drug-addled, bullet-ridden comp to be taught by a lout in a bomber jacket because you 'like, you know, don't believe in private education' makes my liver fizz.

I'm not alone either. Every day the M40 is chock-full of families, their meagre possessions strapped to the roofs of their cars, fleeing from the horror of state education in London. I even have one of them staying in my house right now.

She's not looking for a house here in the Cotswolds. That'll come in time. What she's looking for first is a school where her son can learn to add and subtract in the old-fashioned way with cakes and sweets. Rather than: 'If you stab Johnnie and he loses three pints of blood, how many pints will he have left?'

The problem is that the debate on education cannot be taken seriously when it is opened by an OE like Letwin. Did you see him at the conference last week? Iain Duncan Smith was on the stage, fumbling for his autocue, some berk in a suit three sizes too big was trying to get the osteoporotic audience to its gouty feet every fifteen seconds and there, in the front row, was Eton-educated Letwin, who appeared to be sitting on an electrical socket of some kind.

His face had gone a funny shade of purple and his whole head was rocking about so wildly that at one point I really thought it was in danger of coming off.

Letwin is a funny sort of cove. I sat next to him at dinner once and found him charming, amusing and about 9 inches tall. Also, he is so clever that you get the impression that he's teetering all the time on the edge of slipping into Latin.

Certainly we know by his appearance on *Newsnight* before the last general election that he has a fondness for togas.

None of this matters, though. He could decide to address the National Allotments Society in Aramaic. He could decide to go everywhere for a week on one leg. But everything he does is overshadowed by where he went to school. You just know how his obituary is going to read:

'Mr Oliver Letwin, who was educated at Eton, exploded today. Onlookers described how his head became so full of knowledge that his face turned purple and burst.

'"Stephen Fry told him a little-known fact about Homer and it was the final straw. There simply wasn't enough storage space for any more information in his brain," an Eton-educated doctor said later.

'Mr Boris Johnson, another old Etonian, was devastated. "Ego sum gutted," he said.'

Say someone went to Eton and everyone assumes you're dealing with a sneering man with floppy hair whose elder brother is in the army.

And while we were at school learning about John Donne, the boys at Eton, of course, learnt how to run over members of the working class and how, by speaking very loudly, there is no need for French.

There was also a famous essay written on the subject of poverty by an Eton pupil: 'The father was poor. The mother was poor. The children were poor. The butler was poor. The cook was poor. The projectionist was poor. The chauffeur was poor.' Real world? It stops just outside Windsor and starts again in Slough.

But this caricature isn't true. You can no longer walk through the door simply because your surname is longer than the average chemical symbol.

You need to be very, very bright. And what's more, two of my bestest friends went there in the 1970s. And they've turned out all right(ish).

But the stigma is still there.

We're never told that '*Newsnight* is presented by Jeremy Paxman, who went to Malvern.' And nor does the announcer ever say: 'And now Jonathan Ross, who went to some godforsaken hellhole in Leytonstone.'

My wife has put my son down to go to Eton but this will happen over my dead body and all the bits I've rented out to keep him away from the state schools in Lambeth. I know that he would have a great education for five years but he'd have to spend the next 50 being an old Etonian.

At a comprehensive school he'd be better off because it would be the other way round: five years of being knifed followed by 50 great years of being able to get a dart out of his eye without blubbing.

Sunday 12 October 2003

A Giant Leap Back for Mankind

Like most middle-aged people, I don't know where I was when John F. Kennedy was shot. But I do know where I was when the Air France Concorde crashed into a Paris hotel. And I know where I'll be next Friday: on board the world's only supersonic airliner as it makes its final scheduled flight from New York to London.

As I step off, the temptation will be strong to say: 'That was one small step for a man. But one giant leap backwards for mankind.'

It's hard to think of past examples where human beings had the technology to progress but held back. Maybe AD410, when the Romans pulled out of Britain, but not since. It's not in our nature to snuff out the fire.

We went to the moon and now *Beagle 2* is on its way to Mars. We invented the steam engine and replaced it almost immediately with internal combustion. We went to America in three hours . . . and now we can't any more. It doesn't make sense.

When the British and French governments decided to commission a supersonic jet liner in 1962, the engineers had no clue how such a thing might be achieved. Sure, they had jet fighters up there in the stratosphere, doing more than twice the speed of sound, but these were being flown by young men with triangular torsos in G-suits. The politicians were talking about putting overweight businessmen up there, in lounge suits.

Friends at NASA have told me that the technological challenge of making a Mach-2.2 passenger jet was greater than putting a man on the moon. Those rocket boys get all teary-eyed about their beloved *Apollos*. But when you mention the Concorde, their eyes dry and they nod, slowly and reverentially.

That's because life beyond the 750-mph sound barrier is seriously hostile. There's the friction, which generates so much heat that planes swell by up to a foot.

There's a spot on Concorde's dash that, in flight, is so hot you could fry an egg on it. Then there's the shock wave, a phenomenon of such ferocity that it jams the hydraulics and freezes the controls.

Toward the end of the Second World War, pilots who put their Spitfires into a dive often lost control and could not pull up. They didn't know it at the time but a supersonic shock wave, the source of the sonic boom, was to blame. It sat on the trailing edge of the wings, preventing the ailerons from moving. To get a plane to fly through the sound barrier, this shock wave has to be tamed.

Of course, you can't let the supersonic savagery any-where near those delicate Olympus engines. The air has to be slowed down before it's allowed into the intakes and past the spidery blades.

To make things even more complicated, there's the bothersome business of fuel consumption and reliability.

A typical fighter jet of the 1960s, the Lightning, for instance, was out of juice after about 45 minutes. And it needed up to two weeks of maintenance after a sortie.

Concorde had to fly in that cruel place, where the air is as destructive as a nuclear blast, for 4,000 miles. Then it had to turn around and come home.

The Americans failed with their Supersonic Transport because they aimed for Mach 3 and the exotic materials needed to withstand the heat at this speed weren't commercially available back then. The Russians were more realistic with their Tupolov but it failed because it only had a range of 1,500 miles.

It's worth remembering that Concorde was built by trial and error after error. Men wearing Brylcreem and store coats, endlessly lobbing paper darts down the wind tunnel in Filton.

Make no mistake, Concorde was an extraordinary technological achievement. Almost certainly, one of the greatest.

And not just technically but politically. France and Britain couldn't even agree on how it should be spelt. They finally decided that it should end in an 'e', in the French style, but then Macmillan fell out with de Gaulle and dropped the letter.

It was Tony Benn, the then secretary of state for industry, who solved the matter by declaring it would be 'e' for England, 'e' for Europe and 'e' for *entente cordiale*.

Benn saved Concorde over and over again. He even had to fight the Americans who, in a fit of sour grapes, tried to ban the plane on the grounds that its sonic boom would knock over their cows.

They kicked up such a stink that, bit by bit, the world began to lose confidence in the plane. One by one, the sixteen airlines that had ordered Concorde began to cancel until just two were left: Air France and BOAC.

Knowing that the plane was destined to be a commercial disaster, Benn had to cajole the Treasury and the French until, on 21 January 1976, the scheduled services began. For the first time, paying passengers could fly so fast they could watch the sun rise in the west and arrive in America before they left home.

The cost to the British taxpayer was astronomical: £1.34 billion. Even in today's money, that would nearly get you two Domes.

But, astonishingly, the white elephant became a cash cow. Even though this exotic plane arrived as Freddie Laker began to take the working classes to New York for £59, it regularly flew three-quarters full and made £20 million a year for BA.

From my point of view, in a Fulham flat, Concorde was simply a device that prevented me hearing the second item on the six and ten o'clock news. Twice a night the hum of central London would be drowned by the crackle from those massive engines. And twice a night the entire city would look up. Familiarity never bred indifference.

And then. As I stepped off a Royal Navy Sea King helicopter in York my phone rang to say Concorde had crashed into a Paris hotel.

My reaction was the same as yours. Initial shock that was only slightly lessened when we found out it was an Air France bird and the people on board were not British. Usually, in an accident of this kind, we mourn the people who have died.

But this time it was different. For the first time since Titanic we mourned the loss of the machine itself.

The great white dart. The machine that reminded Londoners twice a day how great we once had been. The plane that was 40 years old but still at the cutting edge of everything. It was not invincible after all.

It never had been, actually. On one BA flight from New York to London one of the engine intakes refused to budge, increasing the drag and therefore the fuel consumption. The captain ignored the advice of his engineer and number two that they should land at Shannon in Ireland to refuel and cruised over the middle of London, arriving at Heathrow with enough juice for 90 seconds more flight. It ran dry while taxiing to the stand. Joan Collins never knew how close she came to being a permanent fixture in the wreckage of what had once been Harrods.

After the Paris crash and 11 September, public confidence in Concorde dried up. I flew on it for the first time last year and couldn't believe how empty it was.

There were lots of things I couldn't believe, actually. Like how small the windows were, and where in such a tiny fuselage they found space for such an extraordinarily well-stocked wine cellar. And how noisy it was in the back. But most of all I couldn't believe the surge of acceleration as it cleared Cornwall and the afterburners took us up past 1,000 mph.

Unless my children become fighter pilots, they'll never feel that surge.

No company or government in the world is currently undertaking serious work on a supersonic airliner. There's talk of Gulfstream building a Mach 2 business jet and there are whisperings about a 'scramjet' plane that could get from London to Sydney in two hours.

In the early 1990s, British Aerospace and Aerospatiale held secret talks about developing a 225-seat aircraft that could get across the Pacific at Mach 2.5. But when the proposed cost of such a thing worked out at £9 billion, they decided to build a double-decker bus instead.

Do you think Columbus would have reached America if he'd concerned himself with the bottom line? Do you think Armstrong would have walked on the moon or Hillary on the top of Everest? Was it profit that took Amundsen to the South Pole or drove Turing to invent the computer?

Compounding the problem is a sense that the First World has pulled so far ahead of the Third, the money would be better spent helping others to catch up. For every pound spent on human advancement, there are a thousand bleeding hearts saying the money could have been spent on the starving in Africa. I see their point.

But what I cannot see is the human thirst for improvement being extinguished by the bean counters. No individual company or country could afford to develop a plane that's significantly better than Concorde, so maybe what's needed is a ring-fenced global fund for the greater good. A fund that undertakes the work business won't touch, hunting the skies for asteroids, searching the seas to find a cure for cancer and fuelling our quest to go faster and faster.

Or maybe the days of mechanical speed are over. Why go to America at the speed of sound when, with an internet connection and video conferencing, you can be there at the speed of light? Why go at all?

Maybe planes are about to follow in the footsteps of the horse. When the car came along, the horse didn't go away. It simply stopped being a tool and became a toy.

A show jumper. A playmate for twelve-year-old girls.

If you can communicate instantly with anyone anywhere the only reason to travel is for fun, for your holidays. And given the choice of doing that at Mach 2 or for £2, I know which I'd choose.

Perhaps, then, this is not a step backwards. Maybe Concorde dies not because it's too fast but because, in the electronic age, it's actually too slow.

Sunday 19 October 2003

What a Wonderful Flight into National Failure

Not much will get me out of bed at 4.30 a.m. in the morning. Especially when I've only climbed into it at 3.30 a.m. But when you've got one of the hundred tickets for the last flight of Concorde . . . I even had a shave.

They seated me right in front of the lavatory, or Piers Morgan, editor of the *Daily Mirror*, as you know him, and between a future hedge investment broker and an American who'd paid $60,000 to be there in some kind of eBay charity auction.

One of the girls flying was completely horrified at the guest list. 'There aren't even any press,' she said. 'Well,' I said, hurting just a little bit, 'that tubby bloke's from the *Independent*. And then there's the *Mail*, the BBC, ABC, NBC, ITN, PA, CNN, Sky, the *Sun*, the *Guardian* and the *Telegraph*.'

'But where's *Hello!*?' That's what she wanted to know.

There'd been talk of Elton John turning up and maybe George Michael too. But in the end all we had was a woman in a wig whom I recognised from a film called *The Stud*, and someone who used to be married to Billy Joel.

The rest? Well there was the chairman of every company from the Footsie, all of them a little bit northern, a little bit florid and, dare I say it, a little bit heavy around the middle.

Despite the weight, Concorde heaved itself into a crystal New York morning at 7.38 a.m. and banking hard – but not so hard that our Pol Roger Winston Churchill champagne fell over – pointed its nose at the rising sun and went home. For the last time.

I was, it must be said, in the mood for a party but this is hard in what's essentially a Mach-2 veal crate. It is possible to leave your seat but you will not be able to stand up properly and then you will have to sit right back down again when the drinks trolley needs to get past.

As we hammered through Mach 1, I asked the hedge-fund man what it was like to go through the sound barrier for his first, and everyone's last time. But he'd nodded off.

The American was deep in monologue with himself. There are no television screens – to save weight – and I'd left my book in my bag.

Concorde was not really designed as a party venue. Unlike the 747 with its larders and its video games, it is a child of the 1950s, a time when you were expected to make your own entertainment. So I did. I lobbed my drink over Morgan.

British Airways were keen that this, the final flight, should not be seen as a wake but rather a celebration of 27 remarkable years.

And to be honest, there was a celebratory mood both in the departure lounge and on the tarmac, where all the pilots of the other early-morning flights sent goodwill messages.

However, at 3.24 p.m. local time, as we dropped back down to Mach 0.98, the mood changed. As everyone realised that we had been the last people to fly faster than the speed of sound without a parachute, it was as though a veil of sadness had been draped over the cabin.

Over London we couldn't help noticing the land-marks of modern Britain. The Dome.

The Millennium Bridge. The traffic jams. The *Mirror* offices. And here we were in the last reminder of how great and innovative we had once been. And we thought: what's going to remind us now?

There was applause as the wheels touched down but in the next 40 minutes, as they unhooked the power and the crowds took photographs, we may as well have been at a funeral. The drink had flowed but the veil, by this time, had become a blanket.

I don't feel sorry for the chairmen who will now need seven hours to get across the Atlantic. It was, after all, their meanness that caused this final flight in the first place.

I don't feel sorry for the nation. It's our own fault that we don't make machines like this any more. I don't even feel sorry for the people who'd struggled to keep Concorde flying these past few years: they'll all get other jobs.

I do, however, feel sorry for the machine itself. It's sitting in its shed now, wondering what it's done wrong. Why did it not fly yesterday and why is there no sense that it will fly today? Why is nobody tinkering with its engines and vacuuming its carpets?

And what was that last flight all about? Why were so many people taking photographs and why, after 27 years, did every single one of Heathrow's 30,000 employees turn out to watch it do what it was designed to do?

I like to believe that a machine does have a heart and a soul. I like to think of them as ordinary people think of dogs. They cannot read or write or understand our spoken words. But they understand what we'd like them to do in other ways. Go left. Go right. Go faster. Sit. Lie.

So go ahead. Think of Concorde as a dog that you've had in the family for 27 years. Think of the way it has never once let you down. And how thrilled it is when you feed it and pet it and take it out for a walk.

And now try to imagine how that dog would feel if you locked it up one night. And never went back.

Sunday 26 October 2003

The Peace Game in Iraq is *Jeux sans Frontières*

You probably thought, as I did, that Iraq had been conquered by the Americans and that Tony Blair had been allowed to take and hold the equivalent of Bournemouth.

In other words, you thought it was a two-country coalition.

But no. Back in February, President George W. Bush announced that despite the best endeavours of the cheese-eating surrender monkeys, he had gathered together 30 like-minded countries and that this 'force for good' would bring peace, goodwill and Texaco to Iraq.

Unfortunately, the 30 countries he had assembled did not include Germany, Russia or China: nations with proud fighting histories and lots of submarines. No. He ended up with an extraordinary collection including Estonia, which did have an army in 1993. But lost it.

No, really; the Estonian army was ordered to capture a Russian military town but the soldiers decided this was an unpleasant way of earning a living and went off, on their own, to fight organised crime instead.

Today Estonia has conscription but most young men get around this simply by not turning up. I don't blame them. What's the point of spending a year playing soldiers when the most frightening thing in your country's military arsenal is the general's dog?

A few years ago the Germans, the Finns and the Swedes had a whip-round and gave their tiny neighbour some uniforms, a couple of patrol boats and a Piper aircraft, but as for guns – well, the Estonians have an Uzi they bought from the Israelis.

In a conflict with Iraq, Estonia would have been a pleasant but fairly useless ally. As would Azerbaijan, which joined the coalition even though it, too, lost its army fourteen months ago and it hasn't turned up yet in Iraq.

President Heydar Aliyev had tried to make life bearable for his troops and even set up a charitable foundation so they could be paid. But as winter drew in last year the soldiers left their barracks, saying they were sick of living without heat and with only an hour of running water a day.

Still, at least Bush could rely on Honduras. Sure, its adult population is the same size as Sheffield's and yes, most people live in houses made from sugar-cane stalks. But there is a modern, well-equipped army and I'm sure the special 'jungle squad' would have been useful in Iraq's desert.

As it turned out, however, the Hondurans never turned up. Nor did the Japanese, who were planning on sending 1,000 peacekeepers. In the wake of last week's big bomb, the Japanese decided it would be better if they just stayed at home. India and Turkey followed suit.

South Korea is also unwilling to commit, but I guess

it's hard to worry about events 10,000 miles away when your next-door neighbour is pointing a thermonuclear weapon through your letter box.

As a result, the team of nations in Iraq looks as though it has been picked by the primary school kid who got to go second. France won the toss and nicked all the big, good players leaving Uncle Sam with the Ukrainians who spend 30 per cent of their GDP on the military (47p), the Romanians who are busy training the new Iraqi police force, the Hungarians who have sent 140 logistics experts, the New Zealanders who have sent some bandages, and the Bulgarians who, presumably, look after the umbrellas.

The Czechs sent 400 policemen but the men have got notes from their mothers and will be going home next month – and it's likely to be the same story with the Italians, who are always up for a fight. Until it starts.

I think everyone with their head screwed on the right way round knew that it would be jolly easy for America's enormous military machine to topple the Ba'ath party in Iraq, even without the Honduran jungle squad and Estonia's second-hand patrol boat.

But we also knew it would be very hard to sort out the mess afterwards. And sure enough, every time the Poles or the Dutch rebuild a water pipe or a power station, half a dozen Talibans drive their Toyotas into it.

It took nearly 80 years to pacify Northern Ireland, where there are only two factions, while in Iraq there are about 120, who can all trace their vendettas back to the Garden of Eden.

To make matters worse, there's not much cohesion among the occupying forces either. One minute a burly Australian comes into your house looking for nuclear weapons, the next a Ukrainian pops round to see if you'd like a job in the police force – and then you get shot in the face by a Shi'ite because a Sunni saw you talking to a Norwegian sergeant about that Bulgarian bird in the wireless section.

Meanwhile, the 130,000 Americans with their Apache gunships and their limitless supply of money are bogged down, trying to work out if Saddam Hussein had anything more dangerous in his chemical cupboard than aspirin.

The war is over, said Bush. Well, you may have stopped playing, matey, but trust me on this: what you have left behind are 187 different teams all playing different games on the same pitch.

Sunday 16 November 2003

The Juries are Scarier than the Criminals

One day, many years ago, when I was a trainee reporter on a local newspaper in the socialist republic of South Yorkshire, a woman telephoned the newsdesk to say her house 'were disgusting'.

I went round, and sure enough it was very dirty and full of equally dirty children, some of whom belonged to the caller.

She wasn't sure which ones exactly, but she was very sure of one thing: cockroaches were burrowing into her head, through her ears, and laying eggs behind her eyes.

She wasn't mad. But she was thick. Thick enough to believe she was thin enough to wear a miniskirt. And thick enough to believe her head was full of maggots when, in fact, it was full of nothing at all.

She wasn't unusual, either. Every day back then I would meet people who knew only to eat when hungry and lash out at anyone who they suspected might be 'looking at them'. People, in other words, with less capacity for logical thought than a dishwasher.

They haven't gone away. Just the other night I was watching a police programme. A young man had been apprehended after he was seen driving erratically and he was, not to put too fine a point on it, incapable of either coherent thought or coherent speech.

When the policeman asked if the car was his, he looked like he'd been asked to explain the atomic properties of lithium. He had the IQ of a daffodil, the conversational ability of a cushion and the intelligence of his mother who, at the time, was standing outside the police car shouting 'Oi, pig!' over and over again.

And yet because this man wasn't a vet or a vicar he could be selected for jury service. Yup, this man, and the woman with cockroach eggs in her forehead, are deemed bright enough to determine the outcome of what might well be a multi-million-pound fraud trial.

Now you may not have noticed, but in between the end of the last parliament and the Queen's speech, when everyone was focused on the big issues of foundation hospitals and university funding, the government was struggling to shove through its new Criminal Justice Bill.

The held view is that trial by jury is the cornerstone of British democracy and if you take it away the whole building will come crashing down.

But actually, when push comes to shove, you don't give a stuff about democracy. If it means getting a few more burglars off the street, damn fairness and decency.

What you want is a system that works. In the wee small hours you can admit that previous convictions should be made known to the court before the case is tried.

You also know that the jury system is a farce.

How can you let a woman who thinks she has insects in her head decide whether it's legal to move a pension fund through the Cayman Islands? In certain parts of

Somerset I suspect that imbecile and embezzle sound exactly the same.

And it's not just fraud either. Back in the olden days when a man was accused of stealing a goat you listened to people who'd seen him do it and made up your mind.

But now you have to have a basic grasp of forensic science.

I can see why Labour MPs are so concerned. They must see many idiots in their surgeries. But the ones who go to a surgery are the gleaming white tip of the iceberg. I'm talking about the sort of people who have no clue what an MP is or what he does; people who you thought existed only in a *Viz* cartoon.

The Tories should be concerned, too, though. I know one upright shires lady who sat on a jury and said afterwards: 'Well, I could tell the little devil was guilty. You could tell the moment he walked into the court.'

A jury is supposed to be made up of your peers, and peers means someone who is equal in standing or rank. Well, I'm sorry, but on that basis the man with the allegedly stolen car on television the other night could only be trusted to try plants.

Terrifyingly, my equal, in terms of someone who writes about cars and occasionally appears on television, is Stephen Bayley. And I wouldn't want to be tried by him either.

At the moment a jury trial has nothing to do with democracy and everything to do with sheer blind luck. But what do we replace it with?

The judge? Ooh, no. Professional jurors? What sort

of person's going to sign up for that? It wouldn't even work, I fear, if we tested the heads of those called.

Because all the bright, intelligent people would pretend to be stupid so they could go home.

I think you may be worried where this is going to end. There's talk at the moment of allowing television cameras into the courts. So how long will it be before the viewers at home are asked to 'press the red button now' and vote? You read it here first.

Sunday 30 November 2003

They're Trying to Frame Kristen Scott Donkey

I've had a horribly busy week and quite the last thing I needed was a directive from the European Parliament that I must get passports for my three donkeys.

I tried to argue that I have no plans to take them abroad, or even out of their paddock, but it was no good. Council Directive 90/426/EEC says that anyone with any horse, mule or donkey must get a passport. At twenty quid a go.

This was going to be a pain in the backside. Geoff, my grey donkey, is so stubborn that he won't even go into his stable, so how in the name of all that's holy was I supposed to get him into one of those photo booths?

I suppose Eddie, who's a playful soul, might have been up for it but then he'd have pulled a silly face every time the flash went off. And let's not forget the beautiful Kristen Scott Donkey who, when the pictures were delivered, would have stood there in tears saying 'they make my nose look too long'.

It turned out that the European Union had thought about this and decided that instead of photographs a simple silhouette drawing would suffice. This makes life easier but I am a trifle worried that silhouettes aren't a terribly good means of identification.

First of all, if I attempted to draw the outline of a

donkey, it would end up looking like a dog. Everything I draw looks like a dog.

My vet says this is no problem so long as I get the markings in the right place.

'But what if my donkey has no markings?' I asked. 'Quite,' he said. Small wonder that Princess Anne called the whole scheme a 'nonsense'.

So what, you might be wondering, is happening here? Why has the EU decided that all equine or asinine species, except those which live in the New Forest or on Dartmoor, must have a photo ID?

Well, and I promise you're not going to believe this, the idea is that each passport will carry details of the animal's medical history. This way you'll know at a glance if it has been fed harmful drugs, should you decide to eat it.

Oh good. So, if one day I suddenly come over all peckish and decide that Geoff's front leg would go well with the veg and gravy, I'll be able to make sure that his previous owner did not feed him a drug that would make me grow two heads.

I think it's worth pausing here for a moment. You see, over the years I have eaten a puffin, a snake, a whale (well, a bit of one), a dog, a crocodile and an anchovy. But I would sooner eat a German than tuck into my donkeys. And I don't think I'm alone on this one either.

For sure, there are problems when a horse dies. You are no longer allowed to bury it in your garden, so you must rely on the local hunt to come and take it away.

But what happens when hunting is banned?

Is the EU saying that we have to break out the carving knife and warm up the sauce?

I don't think so. In Britain we have a line in the sand when it comes to what we will and what we will not put in our mouths. We will eat rats, so long as they're called 'chicken madras'. But we will not eat horses.

Unfortunately, however, the line in the sands of Europe is a little further away.

And consequently those buggers will eat anything.

In France you often find horse on the menu and in Germany, as we discovered last week, it's not against the law to eat your dinner guests. Furthermore, I know they make salami out of the few donkeys in Spain that have not been hurled to their deaths from the nearest tower block.

Over there across the water there is perhaps some argument for equine passports.

Being able to tell if the horse had been on 'horse' at some point in its life would be reassuring. You need to know if the pony's been smacked before it's smoked.

But do you believe for one minute that the farmers of Andalusia are actually going to act on the EU directive? Or do you think the letter will simply be fed to the mule?

That was my first reaction, I must admit. I thought it was a stupid joke and if I did nothing it would go away. But no. It turns out that in Britain, the only country in Europe where we don't eat Mr Ed or Eeyore, local authorities will be employing ass monitors to scour the countryside for unregistered donkeys and horses. And owners will be fined for non-compliance.

Again. Can you see that happening in Europe? I can't. I've seen those massive aquatic vacuum cleaners that Spain calls a fishing fleet pulling into the port of La Coruña and unloading fish about 2 mm long. And there wasn't an EU inspector within a million miles.

I can't even see it working in Germany. The Germans love a rule more than anyone, but when they tried to introduce a similar scheme a few years ago only 50 per cent of the nation's horses were registered. And all the inspectors who were sent out to check on the others mysteriously never came back.

Sunday 7 December 2003

All I Want for Christmas is a Ban on Office Parties

It is traditional at this time of year for newspaper columnists to say how much they despise just about everything to do with Christmas. Sadly, this is not an option for me.

Naturally there are one or two minor irritations. I don't, for instance, like it when someone throws a model aeroplane in your face the moment you walk through the door of Hamleys. And my wife and I have an uncanny knack of buying one another the same thing every year. It's why we have two video cameras and two dogs.

But mostly I get on well with Christmas. My fairy lights work straight out of the box. My tree does not drop needles. I don't eat or drink too much. I like getting long letters in cards from people I haven't seen all year. I enjoy the enforced bonhomie of New Year's Eve.

I find it satisfying to wrap presents. I like turkey curry in February. *The Great Escape* is always worth watching. I don't have any relatives who wet themselves over lunch. I love seeing the children's beaming faces at 5 a.m. I see nothing wrong with Christmas jumpers. I am grateful for my new socks.

I adore Boxing Day drinks parties. I think school nativity plays are funny. I don't get stuck in traffic jams leaving London. I don't get in a panic about last-minute shopping and I don't find it even remotely stressful to be with the family for a few days.

That said, there is one feature of Christmas that fills me with such fear and such dread that I genuinely shiver whenever it is mentioned. It is the damp log in the fire, the mould on the smoked salmon, the advertisement in the Queen's speech. It is . . . the Works Do.

· When I was a schoolboy my mum and dad had a toy factory and, starting in January every year, the staff would each save 10p a week for the annual yuletide knees-up.

By July they would have enough for the prawn cocktail and by September they were dizzy with anticipation about the first glass of Baileys. I never understood why.

I still don't. The notion that you turn off your computer at 6 p.m. and at 6.01 p.m. are making merry with people you don't like very much over a beaker of Pomagne seems odd.

They are not your friends or you would have seen them socially at some point during the year. So why think for a moment that the evening will be anything other than hell?

Christmas in Britain these days is almost completely ruined by the office party.

The streets become full of ordinary people who have suddenly lost the ability to walk in a straight line. And the atmosphere in every restaurant is firebombed by the table of 60 who order food not for its taste but its aerodynamic efficiency.

What's more, for the past week it has been impossible

to get anyone on the telephone because they're either choosing an outfit or finding a restaurant to ruin or having their hair done ready for the Big Day.

I swear some people put more effort into the office party than they do into the family event a few days later. Last year the *Top Gear* Christmas knees-up was organised, as is the way with these things, by someone who is nineteen.

So I ended up in a throbbing basement, looking at my watch every few minutes and thinking: can I really go at 10 p.m.? This year I'm not going at all.

So that's the first thing. Never, ever let the firm's outing be organised by the most junior member of the team because their idea of a good night out – lots of vomit and silly hats – is likely to be far removed from yours.

You think you have nothing to talk about with the man who drives the forklift in the warehouse, but you have even less in common with the office juniors.

Your house plants, for instance, are alive – but you can't smoke any of them.

There is more food in your fridge than booze. You hear your favourite songs when you're in the lift and, while you still like to see the dawn, you prefer to have had a night's kip beforehand.

There is another problem. Wherever the office juniors are, all they talk about is where they're going next. Wherever you are, all you want to do is go to bed. And they say, the day afterwards, 'I'm never going to drink that much again.' You say, 'I just can't seem to drink as much as I used to.'

The second thing about the works party is sex. A survey this week revealed that 45 per cent of people have had it away at the Christmas do. Why? You sit opposite the plump girl for 48 weeks and it never once occurs to you that she is interesting. So how come, after one warm wine, she only needs to put on a paper hat to become Jordan?

Even this year's *Sunday Times* party is likely to be a nightmare, but for a rather unusual reason. You see, the BBC recently said that its staff were to stop writing columns for newspapers. Andrew Marr, John Simpson and our very own John Humphrys are affected.

Me, though? The BBC is not bothered. My opinion, it seems, is irrelevant and worthless. And I'm sure that Humphrys will be duty bound to bring that up.

Sunday 14 December 2003

JEREMY CLARKSON

I KNOW YOU GOT SOUL

Some machines have it and others don't: Soul. They take your breath away, and your heart beats a little faster just knowing that they exist. They may not be the fastest, most efficient, even the best in their class – but they were designed and built by people who loved them, and we can't help but love them back.

For instance,

Zeppelin airships, whilst disastrously explosive in almost every case, were elegant and beautiful bubbles in the air.

The battleships were some of the least effective weapons of war ever built, but made the people who paid for them feel good.

Despite two tragic crashes, the *Space Shuttle* still leaves you with a rocket in your pocket.

Some might dismiss this list as simply being for boys and their toys, but, as Jeremy Clarkson shows, that is to miss the point of what makes the sweep of the Hoover Dam sexier than a supermodel's curves; why the *Princess* flying boat could give white elephants a good name; and why the *Flying Scotsman* beats the Bullet Train every time.

In *I Know You Got Soul*, Jeremy Clarkson celebrates, in his own inimitable style, the machines that matter to us, and tells the stories of the geniuses, boffins and crackpots who put the ghost in the machine.

Jeremy Clarkson

CLARKSON ON CARS

Jeremy Clarkson is the second best motoring writer in Britain. For twenty years he's been driving cars, writing about them and occasionally voicing his opinions on *Top Gear*.

No one on in the business is taller.

Here, he has collected his best car columns and stories in which he waxes lyrical on topics as useful and diverse as:

The perils of bicycle ownership

Why Australians – not Brits – need bull bars

Why soon only geriatrics will be driving BMWs

The difficulty of deciding on the best car for your wedding

Why Jesus's dad would have owned a Nissan Bluebird

… And why it is that bus lanes cause traffic jams

Irreverent, damn funny and offensive to almost everyone, this is writing with its foot to the floor, the brake lines cut and the speed limit smashed to smithereens. Sit back and enjoy the ride.

JEREMY CLARKSON

MOTORWORLD

There are ways and means of getting about that don't involve four wheels, but in this book Jeremy Clarkson isn't interested in them.

Taking himself to twelve countries (okay, eleven – he goes to America twice), Clarkson delves deeply into the hows, whys and wherefores of different nationalities and their relationship to cars.

For instance, why is that Italians are more interested in looking good than looking where they are going? Why do Indians crash a lot? How can an Arab describe himself as 'not a rich man' with four of the world's most expensive cars in his drive? And why have the otherwise neutral Swiss declared war on the car?

From Cuba to Iceland, Australia to Vietnam, Japan to Texas, Jeremy Clarkson tells us of his adventures on and off four wheels as he seeks to discover just what it is that makes our motorworld tick over.

JEREMY CLARKSON

If you enjoyed this book, there are several ways you can read more by the same author and make sure you get the inside track on all Penguin books.

Order any of the following titles direct: